A People's Poetry

HEN BENILLION

Translations by Glyn Jones

seren

seren is the book imprint of
Poetry Wales Press Ltd,
Wyndham Street, Bridgend,
CF31 1EF, Wales

ISBN: 1-85411-178-7

A CIP record for this title is available from
the British Library

*The publisher acknowledges the financial support
of the Arts Council of Wales*

Cover design by Simon Hicks

Printed in Plantin by
Creative Print and Design, Ebbw Vale

Contents

Introduction

The poems I have attempted to translate in this book have been selected from a body of Welsh poetry usually known now as *Hen Benillion*. These words mean in English Old Verses, or Old Stanzas.

I first became aware of this poetry in the early Thirties when I began to take an interest in the Welsh-language literature of my own country. One of the books I bought then was an anthology of Welsh poetry entitled *Y Flodeugerdd Gymraeg* (The Welsh Anthology) edited by the poet and scholar W.J. Gruffydd and published in 1931. This was a selection of Welsh-language poems in the 'free' metres[1] from the sixteenth to the twentieth century and in it, under the heading *Hen Benillion*, I read for the first time some of the poems I have attempted to translate here. Those *penillion* seemed to me amongst the finest things in Gruffydd's anthology.

The following year I came across a recently published paperback of thirty-two pages entitled *Penillion Telyn* (Harp Stanzas). These turned out to be in fact a collection of what I had known until then by their earlier name of *Hen Benillion*, a hundred and forty-five in all, some of which I had previously read in *Y Flodeugerdd Gymraeg*. I was deeply moved afresh by the beauty, liveliness, wit, tenderness and wisdom of this verse and I read and re-read the poems with wonder and delight.

By the time the Second World War had broken out in 1939, Y Clwb Llyfrau Cymraeg (The Welsh Book Club) had been formed. One of its issues was entitled *Hen Benillion*, published in 1940. (*Penillion Telyn*, for a time a common name for the poems, seems now, for a reason I shall refer to later, to have fallen into disuse.) The poems in this book had been collected, chosen, introduced and annotated by T.H. Parry-Williams[2]. This splendid volume contained no fewer than seven hundred and forty-one poems and was, as far as I am aware, the largest collection of *penillion* ever to have been published, although not perhaps the largest ever to have been made. In Parry-Williams's book I found nearly all the stanzas I had previously seen elsewhere, plus a few hundred, many of equal liveliness and beauty, that were new to me. It is from this collection that the great majority of the poems in this

1. The free metres means here not free-verse but poetry without *cynghanedd*. This will be explained more fully later.
2. Later Sir Thomas (1887-1975), poet, essayist, scholar, man of affairs, at that time (1940) Professor of Welsh at the University of Wales, Aberystwyth. A revised edition of *Hen Benillion* was published in 1955.

present book have been translated. I am deeply in Parry-Williams's debt for whatever knowledge I possess of the history of the *Hen Benillion* and for much of what I have to say about them in general in this introduction. I showed him, not long before his death in 1975, a selection of my attempts at translating from his book and received from him a characteristically kind expression of approval and encouragement.

All I have written above amounts to no more than a statement of what I consider to be my single qualification for the task I have undertaken, namely a long-enduring and profound love of these verses, the work, most of them,[3] of our nameless ancestors. It is my hope that even these very inadequate translations will do at least something to suggest the excellence of many of the originals and the pleasure this body of poetry is capable of giving.

I used earlier the expression 'free' metres. As I suggested, these words have, for a Welshman, nothing to do with what we know as 'free verse'. The choice is open to a modern English or American poet of using either free verse (*vers libre*) for his work or the traditional metrical forms of his literature — sonnets, blank verse, rhyming couplets and so on, based on iambic or trochaic feet etc. This choice is of course open equally to the Welsh language poet of today; but a third alternative, one of great antiquity, also exists for him. He can use — very many do — the traditional metres of Welsh classical poetry, the strict metres, the *mesurau caeth* (literally the bound or captive metres) the rules of which were laid down and developed in poetic practice and expounded in metrical treatises over the centuries, and which are still, as I say, in wide use among modern Welsh-language poets. (For a poem using these metres the Chair is awarded annually at the National Eisteddfod of Wales.) The prosodic rules governing the writing of this poetry seem to those hearing of them for the first time (this is my experience, trying to give some idea of them to my English contemporaries) to be insurmountably dogmatic and involved, of daunting and wilful complexity. It is impossible to explain the *mesurau caeth* and their obligatory feature of *cynghanedd* by reference to English poetry because nothing in English poetry resembles the principles on which they are based. I will try to give some indication of the technical skill

---

3. A few of the penillion are attributed to known Welsh poets like Huw Morys, Ellis Wynne, Edward Morus and Ficer Prichard. Ficer Prichard was the Rev. Rhys Prichard whose very popular book *Cannwyll y Cymru* (The Welshman's Candle) was published between 1659 and 1681. Number 258 of these present translations appears in that book.

and knowledge necessary to the writing of the *mesurau caeth* by using as an example part of a *cywydd* (one of the twenty-four metres of classical Welsh poetry) quoted by the Welsh poet Dewi Emrys in his book *Odl a Chynghanedd* (Rhyme and Cynghanedd).

Noson Loergan
(1) Rhoir tegwch awen heno
(2) I lwyndir a bryndir bro;
(3) Gwynion yw llwybrau gweunydd,
(4) A llawr dôl ail lleuer dydd.

It will be apparent I hope, even to those who know no Welsh, that each line of the above, being in the *cywydd* metre, has seven syllables and that the accented syllables of the couplets rhyme with the unaccented. *Cynghanedd*, as it must, occurs in every line. In (1) the *en* of *awen* is repeated in the penultimate syllable of *heno*. In (2) *lwyndir* rhymes with *bryndir* and *bryndir* alliterates with *bro*. In (3) the consonants *G* and *n* in the first half of the line are repeated in the same order in the word *gweunydd* in the second half and in (4) there is a similar correspondence between the sounds *ll*, *r* and *d* in the two halves. And so on, in obedience to the rules of *cynghanedd*, for the fourteen lines that happen to constitute this particular *cywydd*.[4]

A poetry very like this, based on a count of syllables, not of feet, and containing *cynghanedd*, was for centuries for everyone concerned, for poets, listeners, readers, patrons, critics, *Welsh poetry*. This alone. This poetry was the norm, establishment poetry, the poetry that was written down and copied out before books were common, and kept in manuscript over the centuries by those who treasured it. This was the poetry of the *beirdd*, the Welsh poets, until the sixteenth century, and of many poets beyond that date until the present day. Unless we understand the extent in time and the power and authority of the tradition of this type of poetry, the later indifference and resistance to, and even contempt for, the *penillion* is not easy to account for.

In the sixteenth century a new, even revolutionary, development began to take place in Welsh poetry. Dr Thomas Parry, in his *Hanes Llenyddiaeth Gymraeg*[5] tells us that in the Welsh manuscripts written

4.   Those wishing to know more about the *cynganeddion* (plural of *cynghanedd*) will find much information in Gwyn Williams's *An Introduction to Welsh Poetry* (Faber, 1953) and Joseph Clancy's *Medieval Welsh Lyrics* (Macmillan, 1965).
5.   Translated into English by H.I. Bell as *A History of Welsh Literature* and published by Oxford University Press in 1955.

after 1550 poems begin to appear that are different from the poetry of the strict metres I have been describing above. The difference was that these poems were written without *cynghanedd*. It seems possible that poetry of this sort was being composed throughout the previous centuries, concurrently with the strict poetry employing *cynghanedd*, but only by bards of the lowest order, wandering poets, perhaps not much better than beggars, perhaps not unlike the *clerici vagantes*, the wandering scholars of whom and of whose poetry Helen Waddell has written. But unlike the aristocratic poetry in the strict metres, with its elaborate *cynghanedd* and its other devices, this *cynghanedd*-less poetry was not thought worthy of being written down and preserved, and it survived, if it survived at all, not by means of ink and vellum, but on the tongues of the people. But in the second half of the sixteenth century, from 1550 on, this 'free' poetry (i.e. poetry without *cynghanedd*) began to surface and to be written, and to be accepted in Wales as genuine poetry. By that time, after the Act of Union with England and with the Welsh-descended Tudors on the English Throne, relations between the two countries were more cordial than they had been and the 'free' poetry of England might have played its part as an influence on the writing of 'free' Welsh poetry. The new poetry of England at that time was represented in Tottel's *Miscellany* (1557), which included the work of Wyatt and Surrey; the poems of Skelton, Spenser, Sidney and Shakespeare also fall within the century.

But the centuries-old domination of the *cynganeddion* was powerful. As late as 1750, two hundred years after the earliest appearance of the 'free' poetry in manuscripts, Goronwy Owen, a Welsh poet of a high order, after eloquently denying the title of poetry to Milton's *Paradise Lost*, says of Welsh poetry, "without them (i.e. the *cynganeddion*) it were no poetry". And nearly a hundred years after this curious judgment, when the collecting and writing down of the *penillion* had begun, not all literary Welshmen were convinced of their worth. One collector, interested, as many were, in the tunes to which the *penillion* were sung, speaks very disparagingly of the words of the songs ("unstudied productions of the peasantry") and another refers to the verses as "foolish" and describes them dismissively as "this stuff".

Although there are in them here and there traces of *cynghanedd*,[6] the *Hen Benillion* clearly belong to that non-*cynghanedd* tradition

---

6. See among others the originals of translations numbered 5, 17, 40, 72, 81, 191, 247.

which is now firmly established in Welsh poetry. What began general interest in them, the collecting, the writing down and publishing I referred to above, was probably that fashionable interest in things old and things Celtic which was a feature of the eighteenth century, the antiquarian movement in fact associated in England with such figures as Bishop Percy, Thomas Gray, James Macpherson and Thomas Chatterton. The earlier anthologies of Welsh poetry did not include examples of *Hen Benillion* because they were not thought of as *literature*, but, with lullabies, milking and spinning songs, oxen calls and so on, as part of a purely oral tradition. Probably the first Welshman of any critical standing and enlightened literary taste to treat the *penillion* seriously as genuine poetry was Lewis Morris, one of three remarkable brothers — poets, critics, scholars, correspondents, literary impresarios, of the eighteenth century.

Probably the first ever collection of *penillion* to be printed appeared in a book called *Flores Poetarum Britannicorum* which was published in 1710. This was an anthology of Welsh poems employing *cynghanedd* but towards the end of the book were sixty-three moralistic *penillion*. In 1784, in his *Musical and Poetical Relicks of the Welsh Bards*, Edward Jones[7] published a larger collection with some translations into English, that is by the time the volume had reached its fourth edition, in 1825. Edward Jones was of course an experienced musician and his interest was also in the tunes to which the *penillion* were sung. His book, Parry-Williams tells us, was the basis to a large extent for the many collections that followed it. Inevitably the same *penillion* tend to appear in collection after collection. The gathering together and recording of *Hen Benillion* became popular in the eighteenth and nineteenth centuries, with the encouragement of literary societies and *eisteddfodau*. From these collections, many of them still in manuscript, from collections published in magazines, from those which appeared in the volumes I have mentioned and the many others like them, Parry-Williams brought together the seven hundred and forty-one poems of his book.

Since it is difficult to trace the existence of non-*cynghanedd* poetry in Wales before the sixteenth century, we cannot tell how old the earliest of the *penillion* are. But the oldest probably existed as spoken or sung poetry long before they began to be written down. But at last, from being despised and referred to apologetically by literary

---

7. Known as *Bardd y Brenin*, the King's Bard. He was harpist to the Prince of Wales, afterwards George IV.

men for so long, the *Hen Benillion* have now achieved a great measure of critical acceptance, one mark of which is their representation in the *Oxford Book of Welsh Verse* published in 1962. Dr Thomas Parry, the editor, there gives the dates of the nineteen examples he has chosen as "16th - 17th cents". I suppose it must be possible that there are still *penillion* that have escaped the many collectors and remain unrecorded.

I believe I have translated here many of the best known and the most popular of the *penillion*, being guided as to which stanzas belong in those categories by the choice of those anthologists and translators who have dealt with them before me. I include I believe translations of all the verses in W.J. Gruffydd's *Y Flodeugerdd Gymraeg*; the hundred and forty-five in the 1931 *Penillion Telyn* and the nineteen in the *Oxford Book of Welsh Verse*. I am not of course by any means, as I have indicated, the first translator into English of the *penillion*. In our own time, among others, Anthony Conran, Aneirin Talfan, and Gwyn Williams have all undertaken this task. These three are poets and have inevitably selected some of the finest of the verses for translation; but I have not been deterred from attempting the translation of any *pennill* because it has been done before.

Most of the *Hen Benillion*, as will be seen, are short, self-contained stanzas, usually of four lines, having four iambic or trochaic beats to the line and rhyming in couplets, e.g.

> Ar lân y môr mae carreg wastad,
> Lle bûm yn siarad gair â'm cariad.
> O amgylch hon mae teim yn tyfu
> Ac ambell sprigyn o rosmari.

or

> Maent yn dwedyd y ffordd yma
> Nid oes dim mor oer â'r eira;
> Rhois ychydig yn fy mynwes,
> Clywn yr eira gwyn yn gynnes.

Some of the poems consist of a series of such verses. Some stanzas have six lines, some eight, and some have more than eight or nine syllables per line. Internal rhyme is used often, and is an obligatory feature of the stanza form known as Triban Morgannwg or Triban Cyrch, e.g.

12

Peth ffein yw llaeth a syfi,
Peth ffein yw siwgwr candi,
Peth ffein yw myned wedi <u>nos</u>
I stafell <u>dlos</u> i garu.

Some of my English versions lack this internal rhyme as does number 279 in the original Welsh. There are several reasons why I did not attempt to translate all the poems in Parry-Williams's book. Some I omitted, a small number, because I did not care very much for them. Some I could not understand. The metres or the rhyme-schemes of some I found beyond my ability to represent effectively in English, e.g.

Pwy gafodd forwyn<u>dod</u> ei nain yn ddidda<u>nod</u>
Cyn geni ei fam wiw<u>nod</u>, gwir hy<u>nod</u> am h<u>wn</u>?
Pa bryd y bu'r lladd<u>fa</u> fwya' a rhyfedd<u>a'</u>
Er Add<u>a</u> i'r oes ym<u>a</u>? Ymresym<u>wn</u>.

Some, and in this class were stanzas which seemed to me amongst the most splendid,[8] I omitted because I failed completely to suggest in my verse translations the force and beauty of the originals. Stanzas relying on puns and such devices for their effect I found untranslatable. Some stanzas were repetitive, similar to others I had already translated and these I usually passed over. In a chain of verses on the same subject I felt sometimes that one stanza was outstanding and representative, and that the rest were repetitious, diminishing the effect of the best rather than enhancing it, so these too I did not attempt. In making such a choice I have perhaps perpetuated a process of selection that had operated previously in the history of the *penillion*. A *pennill* is a stanza and it seems likely that some of those we now have were once, not individual verses, but part of longer poems by forgotten country poets. The stanza that survived, while the rest of the poem disappeared, did so presumably because of its vividness, or aptness, or beauty, and of course its completeness and self-sufficiency.

Although I have stayed throughout as close as possible to the metres and rhyme-schemes of the originals, some of my renderings turn out to be less translations than what the translator of an English hymn into Welsh would call in our hymn-books an *efelychiad*, i.e.

---

8. e.g. 'Rhyd y bompren grwca', from *Penillion Telyn*. A prose translation would go something like this — "crooked-wooden-bridge ford, whom did I see going through it?" "Your lover, colour of thorn flowers, like fine cambric from India."

an imitation. I felt often that a sort of perversity existed in the vocabulary of either English or Welsh. What I mean is that key words and words very frequently used in the *penillion* — *calon, cariad, mynwes, dwyfron, tonnau, cusan, tannau, lleuad, adar, carreg, dwylo,* — are all disyllables with the accent on the first syllable. Often these were words that seemed to come at the ends of the lines and so required feminine rhymes. How much easier for a translator if their English equivalents had been other than the monosyllabic heart, love, breast, breast (again), waves, kiss, strings, moon, birds, rock and hands. Another difficulty arose sometimes through the language used by the young man to address his sweetheart. It appears natural enough that a Welsh lover should think of his girl as *lliw'r manod* (snow-drift white) or *lliw'r eira gwyn* (colour of white snow) or *lliw blodau'r drain* (colour of thorn flowers). But the English equivalents of some of these endearments, *lliw wy* for example, or *lliw blawd,* seem somehow inappropriate and ambiguous. Eggs and flour, particularly eggs (brown in colour, white, green and spotted) hardly seem images suitable for the language of passion and romance when translated into English. *Fenws* (Venus) too, seems much more natural in Welsh than in English.

The singers or speakers in the *penillion* must be thought of as both men and women, sometimes children, sometimes even animals. A man and a woman might express a similar idea from the point of view of their respective sex, as in numbers 213 and 214. The language of the *penillion,* as one would expect of poems that arose from and remained so long part of an oral tradition, is the language of ordinary speech. It is simple and often powerful, but can be repetitive and limited. The pronunciation is often colloquial (*llestar* for written or literary *llestr, sicir* for *sicr, cellwer* for *cellwair* and so on), and English-sounding words are sometimes introduced, e.g. *batel, lysti, wantan, staes* (stays), *ffri* (free). I felt these practices justified my own occasional use of colloquialisms and slang in my translations, of words like kidding, boggle, quid, posh, scarper, dig (notice, approve of) and gammy (bent or crooked). Frequently we find stanzas beginning with the same words, with phrases like *Tri pheth ...* (Three things), *Tro yma d'wyneb ...* (Turn your face here), *Pe bawn i ...* (If I were) and so on. It is interesting that the opening of successive stanzas with the same words is a feature also of some of the oldest Welsh poetry, of the sixth century *Gododdin* and the ninth century Llywarch Hen/Heledd cycle.

The only reference to what one might call industry I have come across in the *penillion* is one to the "paper-mill" in verse 232. Their subjects are the loves, sorrows, enjoyments, follies, jealousies, vanities, oddities, satisfactions, of an entirely rural community, of a pre-industrial era, the feasts, the fairs, the crops, the changing seasons, the creatures, the pre-romantic joy in nature which did not appear to encompass a liking for mountains.[9] Praise, satire and melodrama are all present in them. Many praise the harp and harpists. Although one collector uses the word in describing it, this is not pastoral poetry in any modern sense. The poets who produced it were nearer to Clare than to Milton, and the poetry was not transmuted by poetic convention. They were not scholarly or cultivated visitors from the town, poetic 'country lovers' but the people on the spot, smiths, shoemakers, cobblers, glovers, tailors, shepherds, weavers, and so on, the craftsmen who are mentioned in the poems. Amateurs with another job, producers of good cloth or sound horse-shoes (one hopes) by day and of small and perhaps perfect works of art by night. All the references in any particular *pennill* would be entirely meaningful only to a member of the community for which that *pennill* had been composed. I suppose we shall never know what was so special about the buff breeches of Huw Hwmffre of Nantlle (number 193), or the riding get-up of the wife of Cwmcloch (number 205), or who the little man was met with near Henllan Bridge (number 199). One character we *do* know about from other sources is the famous *Marged fwyn ach Ifan* of number 207.

I suppose the English poets that one would expect to come to mind during translation would be Herrick, Blake, Housman, W.H. Davies, perhaps Idris Davies. Numbers 137 and 141 did indeed in different ways recall Blake and number 77 one of the songs of Shakespeare, but the verses have never seemed to me to resemble closely any English poetry, not even the folk poetry in Geoffrey Grigson's *Faber Book of Popular Verse* (Faber, 1971). Their uniqueness has always been to me one of their chief attractions, they provide a type of *frisson* not readily encountered from any other source.

The question must arise — for what purpose was this great body of verse produced? Like much Welsh poetry its function was social, it was intended to serve a community. We have more than one account, in the books of travellers, novelists and others, of the

---

9. See number 152. Other verses in Parry-Williams express a similar dislike.

nosweithiau llawen, the happy evenings, that used to take place in earlier centuries in rural, pre-industrial Wales. These gatherings were held, one supposes, in private houses in the villages and small towns, in farms and in taverns, although some of the *penillion* are anti-drink. The painter J.C. Ibbetson (1759-1817) has a water-colour of *penillion* singing in Bangor being held in the open air.[10] Presumably the time and place of these gatherings were circulated beforehand and people came together after work to dance, sing, listen, chat, eat and drink and enjoy themselves. We are told that it was not uncommon in eighteenth-century Wales to meet people who could recite or sing to the harp hundreds of *penillion* from memory, and this must have been a necessary accomplishment since the verses are short and it would certainly require knowledge of a few hundred to sustain an evening's entertainment.[11] One chain of *penillion* I have attempted (number 2) is about a competition between two rival groups of singers and these opponents often represented different parishes or even counties. The adulation of the popular harpist (numbers 38-43) recalls in intensity, if not in territorial extent, the pop-star idolatry of today. The *pennill* became the poor man's *cywydd,* the two the products of different poetic traditions and of different classes, but having in common an element of performance and social purpose.

But whether all the stanzas we have now were intended for singing to the harp is perhaps doubtful. Indeed number 176 in Parry-Williams refers to not to singing the *penillion* but to *reciting* them. And perhaps the old man in number 1 here is a speaker, not a singer. Some no doubt survived, not because they were associated with a tune and with being sung to harp music, but because they embodied some piece of wisdom, or expressed neatly a widely-held belief or the fruit of experience, "enriching", as one writer has it, "the public memory with maxims". These would undoubtedly be quoted when the appropriate occasion arose, as proverbs, saws, catch-phrases, verses from the Bible and even limericks are. Some lines of the penillion are indeed almost proverbial, as — The one who comes from afar will be listened to: Useless to wash the feet of the ducks:

10. William Leathart, in *Welsh Penillion,* published in London in 1825, tells us that singing *penillion* was finished in South Wales by that date but he gives us a list of "harp meetings" being held in London each week from Monday to Friday, as "Friday — The Bell, John Jones, W. Prichard, harper. At David Jones's, Pickle Herring Stairs, Southwark, H. Thomas".
11. Edward Jones says the meetings could go on all day and even all the week and the number of verses some people had memorised was "perhaps thousands".

Don't fear the waves before meeting the sea: It's hard to plait the water of the river — and so on.

The fact, as we may suppose, that the *penillion*, when they were sung, were sung openly for pleasure in periods of leisure and recreation at mixed public gatherings of friends and neighbours, means certain limitations of subject matter and treatment probably existed for authors and performers. Very few of the *penillion* have anything to say about religious experience, although moral precepts are not uncommon. Very few are excessively bawdy or indecent. Very few again are concerned with social criticism, what we now call protest. The only one to arise, as far as I can see, from anything approaching a theoretical view of poverty and riches is number 274. If these country people did feel any resentment at their social lot, if they saw the squire, say, as their oppressor and exploiter, they did not express their feelings in their public singing gatherings. They contented themselves perhaps with stanzas that made mild fun of his wife or daughter or relatives (numbers 125, 201, 205). Indeed some of the authors of the *penillion* seem to have been themselves not craftsmen or tenant farmers but of the class that inherited land (number 264). We must remember however that the stanzas we are likely to see in print now are very far from being the whole body of the *Hen Benillion*. Even Parry-Williams's extensive collection is only a choice made from the thousands he must have read in the printed books, magazines, manuscripts and so on that he lists. What we read now are selections of selections of those *that happen to have survived* and been recorded. How much censorship, conscious and unconscious, has gone on over the years since the first collection of *penillion* appeared I do not know, but it seems probable that, from the time of the earliest collectors, what has appeared unsuitable, for whatever reason, for printing and publishing, would be rejected.

In this introduction I have said nothing about one aspect of the *Hen Benillion* that is of the greatest interest and importance to many, I mean the question of the tunes to which they were set, and the art of *canu penillion*, the singing of *penillion*. This is a large, and for someone as musically illiterate as myself, an intimidating matter and far beyond the scope of a modest introduction of this sort. My aim in this book has been merely to suggest to those without Welsh the pleasure to be had from these simple Welsh poems in the hope that they might feel that the learning of the language of the immeasurably superior originals might be worthwhile.

'Said the Old Man ...'

1

Dwedai hen ŵr llwyd o'r gornel,
   'Gan fy nhad mi glywais chwedel,
A chan ei dad y clywsai yntau,
Ac ar ei ôl mi gofiais innau'.

1

The grey old man said from the corner,
'I heard stories from my father,
And from *his* father he had heard them.
After my father I recall them'.

Ymryson Canu

'Os wyt ti am ymryson canu,
Cais dy stôl ac eistedd arni;
Mi ymrysonaf dan y bore,
Cyn y rhoddaf iti'r gore.'

'Mae gen innau o benillion
Rif y gwlith ar ddolydd gleision;
A phe bae'n bleser gennyf ganu,
Gwnawn i ti a'th gwmni dewi.'

'Tebyg yw dy lais yn canu
I gog mewn craig yn dechrau crygu,
Dechrau cân heb ddiwedd arni,
Harddach fyddai iti dewi.'

'Tebyg yw dy lais di'n canu
I hen fuwch pan fo hi'n brefu,
Neu gi dall yn clepian cyfarth
Wedi colli'r ffordd i'r buarth.'

'Tebyg iawn wyt i'r dylluan;
O bren i bren bydd honno'i hunan
A phob 'deryn yn ei phigo,
Tebyg iawn wyt tithau i honno.'

'Os tebyg ydwyf i'r dylluan,
Sydd o bren i bren ei hunan,
Tebyg iawn wyt tithau i'r gigfran,
Hyd y creigiau bydd hi'n crowcian.'

Singing Contest

'If for a singing match you'd care
Just find and sit upon your chair;
I can cap your songs till morning,
You'll not beat me, so take warning.'

'The verses that I know and knew
Are numerous as green meadow dew;
And should I please to sing my stanzas
You and your party'd have no answers.'

'A cuckoo in a rock I heard —
Your voice recalls that croaking bird,
Starting some song that has no ending.
Best thing for your voice is resting.'

'*Your* voice, when you start singing,
Is some old cow's that won't stop mooing;
A yapping dog's who fails to find
His farmyard home because he's blind.'

'From branch to branch a certain fowl
Flies alone, and that's the owl,
Pecked at by all the other birds,
And that's what *you're* like, in few words.'

'If I am like that owl who's known
To fly from branch to branch alone,
You're very like that thing whose haven
Is up the crags — the croaking raven.'

Plentyndod ac Ieuenctid

3

'Merch i bwy wyt ti, lliw'r manod?'
'Merch fy nhad a'm mam o briod.'
'O ba wlad y daethost allan?'
'O wlad fy nhad a'm mam fy hunan.'

4

Gyda'r nos daw'r tŷ yn dywyll,
Gyda'r nos daw golau'r gannwyll,
Gyda'r nos daw diwedd chware,
Gyda'r nos daw tada adre.

5

Da gan adar mân y coedydd,
Da gan ŵyn feillionog ddolydd,
Da gen i brydyddu'r hafddydd
Yn y llwyn a bod yn llonydd.

6

Peth braf yw haf a hawddfyd,
Peth braf yw ysgawn iechyd,
   Peth braf yw arian yn y pwrs,
Peth braf yw cwrs yr ienctid.

7

Mi fynnaf ffedog liain main,
   Fel 'roes fy nain i Sionad;
Mynnaf ardysau wstyd mân
   A 'sanau o wlân y ddafad,
Ac esgid ledr i siwtio 'nhroed,
A mab o'm hoed yn gariad.

Childhood and Youth

3

'Whose daughter are you, snow-drift white?'
'Father's and mother's and marriage rite.'
'Out of what country did you journey?'
'My father's and my mother's country.'

4

When comes night the house falls darkened,
When comes night the rooms are candled,
When comes night then play is past,
And dada's all come home at last.

5

Little birds all love their woodlands,
Little lambs their clovered lowlands,
In summer days I'm not averse
Up the woods, to writing verse.

6

A fine thing — summer leisure,
A fine thing — health and pleasure,
A fine thing is a purse with cash
And youth's brave dashing manner.

7

I'd like an apron of fine cloth
    Like Sionad had from Grandma;
Pretty worsted garters too
    And sheeps-wool stockings after,
And leather boots to suit my feet
And a lad my age for lover.

8

Mae bachgen yn Llanegryn yn 'sgolor doeth a llon,
A fedr fesur tiroedd a gwneuthur deial gron.
Gall fesur Cadair Idris yn gywir yn ei lle,
Nid oes yn Sir Feirionnydd yr un o'i debyg e.

9

Titw pytaten, i ble'r aeth dy fam?
Hi aeth i lygota, a chafodd beth cam.
Gwraig y tŷ nesaf a'i biwsiodd hi'n frwnt,
A churodd ei dannedd yng nghaead y stwnt.

8

A boy there in Llanegryn, a scholar wise and sound,
Can measure out the landscapes and makes sundials
    round.
The height of Cader Idris he measures fair and
    square,
Of brainy boys in Meirion — he has no equal there.

9

'Pussy Potato, where is your Mam gone?'
'Out mousing she went, and was soon put upon.
That woman next door, she abused her, poor cat,
So that Mam bashed her teeth on the spout of
    the vat!'

Caru

10

Nani, Siani, Lowri, Sioned,
Liwsi, Cadi, Mali, Marged,
Beti, Susi, Grasi, Neli,
Sali, Weini sy dda genni.

11

Caru 'Nghaer a charu 'Nghorwen,
Caru'n Nyffryn Clwyd a Derwen,
Caru 'mellach dros y mynydd,
Cael yng Nghynwyd gariad newydd.

12

Mi eis i garu dros y mynydd
Yn fy 'sanau gwynion newydd.
Wrth fynd trwy hen gorsydd gwlybion
Cefais bâr o 'sanau duon.

13

Ar y ffordd wrth fynd i'r farchnad,
Cwrdd a wnes â'm hannwyl gariad.
Cyntaf gair a gawn i ganddi,
'Pa bryd y cawn ni'n dau briodi?'

'Pan fo'r fedwen las yn tyfu
Â'i brig i lawr a'i bôn i fyny,
A'r coed rhos yn dwyn afalau,
Dyna'r pryd y cewch chwi finnau.'

14

Pan brioda Siôn a minnau
Fe fydd cyrn ar bennau'r gwyddau,
Ieir y mynydd yn blu gwynion,
Ceiliog twrci fydd y Person.

Courting

10

Nani, Siani, Lowri, Sioned,
Liwsi, Cadi, Mali, Marged,
Beti, Susi, Grasi, Neli,
Sali, Weini — you're all lovely!

11

Courting in Chester and in Corwen,
Courting in Dyffryn Clwyd and Derwen,
Up the mountain courting further,
Finding in Cynwyd a new lover.

12

I went across the mountain courting,
My new white stockings I was wearing.
After all the bogland's soakings
I'd got a pair of pitch-black stockings.

13

On the road one market day
I met my sweetheart on her way.
These the first words that she said —
'Tell me, when shall we two wed?'

'When the green birch tree has grown,
Roots and branches, upside down;
When the rose-bush brings forth apples —
Then we'll wed like other couples.'

14

When John and I'll be newly-weds
Geese will have horns upon their heads,
White-plumed grouse will form a flock,
The priest will be a turkey-cock!

15

Do, bûm ganwaith yn dy garu,
Feinir wen, a thithau'n gwadu;
Ond yn awr, mae'n rhaid cyfadde',
Beth a wnaet pe gwadwn inne?

16

Bachgen coch a'm gwnaeth i'n glaf;
Bachgen coch, pa beth a wnaf?
Bachgen coch a'm rhodd mewn penyd,
Bachgen coch all safio 'mywyd.

17

Hen wraig fach ar fin y mynydd
A chanddi eneth laweth lonydd.
Pwy debygech, ddaeth i'w charu? —
Clochydd Llangwm wedi meddwi.

18

Tri pheth sy gas wrth garu —
Oeri traed a cholli cysgu,
Tan y bargod yn dal defni,
A'r ferch yn chwerthin yn y gwely.

19

Cael yr ysgol ar y pared,
Cael y ffenestr yn agored,
Cael y gwely wedi'i gyweiro,
Methu cael f'anwylyd ynddo.

20

'Fy nghariad annwyl, dyner, glws,
Tyrd i'r ffenest' neu i'r drws
Mae gŵr ifanc dan y pared
Yn dymuno cael dy weled.'

15

Yes, a hundred times I've loved
You, darling, but you disapproved;
Now what would *you* do if I said
I disapproved of you, and fled?

16

Redhead has made me ill — it's true;
Redheaded boy, what shall I do?
Redhead's put me in the way.
Redhead alone can save the day.

17

Up the mountain an old mother
Lived with a quiet captive daughter.
Who came to court her, do you think?
Llangwm's sexton, the worse for drink!

18

Courting, three things are hard to take —
Cold feet, and half the night awake,
While her eaves leak on my head,
And she, the girl, laughs up in bed.

19

The ladder leans against the thatch;
The bedroom window's off the latch;
Inside the room the bed's prepared;
But where's the girl who claimed she cared?

20

'Oh gentle girl whom I adore,
Come to your window or your door.
A young lad longs here in this place
Below your wall, to see your face.'

'Yn wir ni chodaf i o'm gwely
I siarad gwagedd drwy'r ffenestri.
Mae'r gwynt yn oer, a minnau'n dene,
Dowch yn gynt neu sefwch gartre.'

21

Os daw 'nghariad yma heno,
Mi wna' 'n ddigon mawr ohono;
Fe gaiff gadair wellt i eiste,
Wrth ei glun eisteddaf inne.

22 [582]

Propor gorff, ai ti sydd yma?
Dod dy draed ar lawr yn ara',
Gwylia daro wrth yr ysgub,
Ysgafn iawn y cwsg fy modryb.

23 [632]

Mi allaf, Gaenor, dy briodi
Os caf i ganpunt hefo thýdi;
Ac fe gei dithau efo minnau
Ryw ddau neu dri o hen geffylau,
A llawer iawn o ddanedd ogau.

24

Siân sydd fwyn, a Siân sydd lân,
A Siân sydd gyflawn gofled;
Pe cawn i Siân rhwng braich a bron,
Mi wasgwn hon yn galed.

'I'll never leave this bed I'm in
To talk your rubbish. I am thin —
And this wind's as cold as clay.
Come earlier, lad, or stay away.'

21

If my darling comes tonight
He shall have all for his delight —
Sit in the wicker chair, at peace;
Beside his knee shall be my place.

22

My sweet of body, have you come?
Mind how you tread, no noise, be dumb.
There's clangour in that sweeping-brush!
My aunt sleeps light, so sweet one, hush.

23

Just bring me Gaenor, as I've said,
A hundred pounds — then we can wed.
My own fair share to you shall be
Two ancient nags, or maybe three,
And heaps of harrow-teeth for free.

24

Siân is gentle, Siân is fair,
    So debonair an armful;
Siân in between my arms and breast,
    Hard pressed, would be delightful.

25

Curo y bûm yn anial ffest
　Yn ffenest' onest eneth,
Methu'n wir ei deffro hi
　A wnaeth i mi fyn'd ymeth.
Bydd yr hin yn rhewi'r haf
　Pan geisiaf nesaf nosweth.

26

Titrwm, tatrwm, Gwen lliw'r wy,
　Ni alla' i'n hwy mo'r curo;
Mae'r gwynt yn oer oddi ar y llyn;
　Lliw blodau'r dyffryn, deffro.
Chwyth y tân i gynnau toc, —
　Mae hi'n ddrycinog heno.

27

Fe ellir rhodio llawer ffair,
　A cherdded tair o orie,
A charu merch o lawer plwy',
　Heb wybod pwy sydd ore:
Mae'n anodd dewis derwen deg
　Heb arni freg yn rhywle.

28

Os 'nghariad ddaw 'ma heno
　I guro'r gwydyr glas,
Rhowch ateb gweddus iddo,
　Na ddwedwch ddim yn gas, —
Nad ydyw'r ferch ddim gartref
　Na'i h'wyllys da'n y tŷ;
Llanc ifanc o blwyf arall
　Sydd wedi mynd â hi.

25

In eager haste I went one night
    To tap a bright girl's window;
But soon I quit, because the lass
    Stayed dozing on her pillow;
There'll be skating in July
    Next time I try you, bright-brow.

26

Rat-tat, rat-tat, Oh, egg-white Gwen,
    I can't go on just tapping;
This wind is bitter off the lake —
    Oh, wake, my lily-white darling;
Quick, blow the fire up, make it bright —
    Out here this night is freezing!

27

One can court girls at many fairs,
    Can walk in pairs in plenty;
Love many a wench and not decide
    Who'll be your bride, your beauty —
It's hard to choose an oak without
    Some branch or sprout that's faulty.

28

Now if tonight my sweetheart
    Should tap the window pane,
Give him a courteous answer —
    Nothing to cause him pain.
The girl he seeks is absent
    Her good-will's not at home,
For from another parish
    The lad she'll wed has come.

29

'R wy' 'n caru tair yn ffyddlon
 chelwydd drwy lythyron;
   Ond pan fwy' 'n gorfod mynd i ffair,
Mae un o'r tair yn ddigon.

Os yn y ffair cyferfydd
Y tair, bydd arnaf g'wilydd
   O'u gweld hwy gyda golwg swrth
Yn ffoi oddi wrth ei gilydd.

30

Mae Ffair y Borth yn nesu,
Caf deisen wedi ei chrasu,
   A chwrw poeth o flaen y tân,
A geneth lân i'w charu.

31

Peth ffein yw llaeth a syfi,
Peth ffein yw siwgwr candi,
   Peth ffein yw myned wedi nos
I stafell dlos i garu.

32

O neithiwr a neithiwr a neithiwr yn hwyr,
Ow, neithiwr a neithiwr a'm lladdodd yn llwyr;
Y fuwch heb ei godro a'r tŷ heb ddim llaeth,
A digio fy nghariad, — 'r oedd hynny'n saith waeth.

33

Mae 'nghariad i 'leni fel gwynt o flaen glaw,
Yn caru'r ffordd yma a charu'r ffordd draw.
Ni châr cywir galon yn gariad ond un;
Y sawl a gâr lawer gaiff fod heb yr un.

29

I am the faithful lover
Of three, by lies and letter;
    But on each fairday one of these,
Not three, would suit me better.

For I should not feel clever
If my three girls should ever
    In the fairground, face to face,
Meet — and then race asunder!

30

Borth Fair is now approaching
Where hot cakes will be baking;
    Mulled beer before the fire I'll taste,
And find a girl's waist for squeezing!

31

Wild strawberries are lovely
With milk — so's sugar candy,
    And going to her room at night
To court my flower-white beauty.

32

Oh, last night and last night and last night quite late,
Oh, last night and last night it was sealed my fate!
The cow never milked, in the house not one tot,
And my sweetheart she pouted — that's worse than
    the lot.

33

My sweetheart this year is like wind before rain —
He loves far and near, but what does he gain?
Those constant of heart they love truly but one,
And he who loves many ends up having none.

34

Mi fûm yn dy garu yn fawr ac yn fawr;
Ni allwn fod hebot un munud nac awr.
Yr awron 'r wy' 'n caru un arall yn fwy;
Mi allwn fyw hebddi am flwyddyn neu ddwy.

35

Yn hen ac yn ieuanc, yn gall ac yn ffôl,
Y merched sy'n gwra, a minnau ar ôl;
Paham y mae'r meibion i'm gweled mor wael,
A minnau cyn laned â'r merched sy'n cael?

36

Fel 'r oeddwn i neithiwr yn sefyll yn syn
Yn ffenest' fy nghariad, mi welwn beth gwyn.
Mi dynnais fy nghleddyf, gan feddwl rhoi brath;
Na bo ond ei grybwyll, 'd oedd yno ond y gath.

37

Ffarwél i godi'n fore, ffarwél i fwydo'r moch,
Ffarwél 'r wyf yn ei roddi i'r mab â'r wasgod goch.
Mi droais hwnnw heibio, — on'd gwiwlwys oedd
    y gwaith?
'R wy' 'n caru'n awr o galon y mab â'r wasgod fraith.

34

I once loved you greatly, so greatly I'd say
I couldn't be parted one minute or day.
I love someone better than you now, and laugh
At absence from her for a year and a half.

35

Old, young, wise and foolish, I see womankind
All landing a lover, while I'm left behind.
Why, why, am I thought plain, and can't get a man?
I'm sure I'm as pretty as those girls who can.

36

Last night by her window I had a great fright,
For as I stood waiting I saw something white!
I pulled out my broad-sword, intending to kill —
'Miaou', cried the cat, jumping down from the sill!

37

Goodbye to early rising, and seeing the pigs are fed,
And goodbye to that fellow whose waistcoat was
        bright red;
I sacked him and enjoyed it — a job without a fault!
The chap I love at present, his waistcoat's
        pepper-and-salt!

Telynau a Thelynorion

38

Llawer gwaith y bu fy mwriad
Gael telynor imi'n gariad,
Gan felysed sŵn y tanne,
Gyda'r hwyr a chyda'r bore.

39

Dyn a garo grwth a thelyn,
Sain cynghanedd, cân ac englyn,
A gâr y pethau mwyaf tirion
Sy yn y nef ymlith angylion.

40

Yr un ni charo dôn a chaniad
Ni cheir ynddo naws o gariad;
Fe welir hwn, tra byddo byw,
Yn gas gan ddyn, yn gas gan Dduw.

41

Mwyn yw peraidd leisiau'r adar
Ar y clyw ar fore claear;
Gwell gen i yw clywed englyn
Mewn acenaid gyda'r delyn.

42

Da gan ddiogyn yn ei wely
Glywed sŵn y droell yn nyddu,
Gwell gen innau, dyn a'm helpo,
Glywed sŵn y tannau'n tiwnio.

Harps and Harpists

38

Many times have I thought over
Having a harpist for a lover,
Since the strings' sound has such sweetness
Both at dawn and evening's darkness.

39

Who loves the harp, and melody,
Englyn, song, and harmony,
Loves gentlest things heard in those revels
Held in heaven amongst the angels.

40

One unmoved by tunes and singing
Must be quite bereft of loving;
Throughout his life that fellow'll never,
Not with man or God, find favour.

41

Sweet to hear on some mild morning
The gentle voice of song-birds singing;
What I love best to hear's some bardic
Englyn set to sweet harp music.

42

The spinning-wheel — how sweet it drones
When heard from bed, thinks lazy-bones.
God help me — I am just as wretched,
With sweet harp music I'm besotted.

43

'Pe bai gwallt fy mhen yn felyn,
Fe wnâi dannau yn eich telyn.
Ond gan nad yw yn wir ond gwinau,
Rhaid i'ch telyn fod heb dannau.'

Ni raid i'm telyn fod heb dannau
Gan faint o goludd sy'n y siopau,
Pe bai blewyn byth heb dyfu
Ar eich pen chwi, Siwsan Sosi.

43

'My hair yellow — then I'd look sharp
To make strings from it for your harp.
It's brown, so you must be content
With a stringless instrument.'

'My harp need never lack for strings
While such gut in the butcher's swings
And should your head grow no more hair,
Saucy Sue, my strings hang there.'

Gwewyr Cariad

44

Mi ddymunais fil o weithiau
Fod fy mron o wydr golau,
Fel y gallai'r fun gael gweled
Fod y galon mewn caethiwed.

45

Fe gwn yr haul pan ddêl boreddydd,
Fe gwn y tarth oddi ar y dolydd,
Fe gwn y gwlith oddi ar y meillion,
Gwae fi, pa bryd y cwn fy nghalon?

46

Dod dy law, on'd wyt yn coelio,
Dan fy mron, a gwylia 'mriwio;
Ti gei glywed, os gwrandewi,
Sŵn y galon fach yn torri.

47

Mi wrthodais, ffôl yr oeddwn,
Ferch a garai'r tir a gerddwn,
Ac a gerais, do, 'n garedig,
Ferch a'm gwerthai am ychydig.

Do, mi welais heddiw'r bore
Ferch a gawn pan fynnwn inne,
Ac a welais, do, brynhawn,
Ferch a garwn ac nis cawn.

48

O f'anwylyd, cyfod frwynen,
Ac ymafael yn ei deupen;
Yn ei hanner tor hi'n union
Fel y torraist ti fy nghalon.

Pains of Love

44

So that my heart you might see
Chained in its sad captivity,
I have often wished, my lass,
My breast were made of clear glass.

45

At dawn the sun will rise up yellow,
The mist will rise from off the meadow,
And from the clover dew will rise.
Woe's me, when will my heart arise?

46

You don't believe? Let your hand rest
Here on the wound beneath my breast;
You shall hear that sound the aching
Heart makes — listen! — when it's breaking.

47

I gave up, for no good reason,
A girl who loved the ground I trod on;
And I worshipped as my lover
A girl who'd sell me down the river.

Yes, I saw the girl this morning
Who, if I whistled, would come running:
This afternoon, her head held high,
The girl I worship passed me by.

48

Pluck that bullrush where it stands,
Take both ends, love, in your hands:
Break it in two, split it apart
The way you broke my faithful heart.

49

Ni bu ferch erioed cyn laned,
Ni bu ferch erioed cyn wynned;
Ni bu neb o ferched dynion
Nes na hon i dorri 'nghalon.

50

Pan own i'n rhodio glan môr heli,
Gwelwn wylan o liw'r lili
Ar y traeth yn gwasgu'i godre
Oedd wedi gwlychu yn y tonne.

Mi roes fy mhen i lawr i wylo,
Fe ddaeth yr wylan ataf yno.
Mi roes lythyr dan ei haden
I fynd at f'annwyl siriol seren.

51

Os collais i fy nghariad gorau,
Colli wnelo'r coed eu blodau,
Colli'u cân a wnelo'r adar,
Duw a gadwo ffrwyth y ddaear.

52

Llun y delyn, llun y tannau,
Llun cyweirgorn aur yn droeau:
Dan ei fysedd, O na fuasai
Llun fy nghalon union innau!

53

Dacw lwyn o fedw gleision,
Dacw'r llwyn sy'n torri 'nghalon;
Nid am y llwyn yr wy' 'n ochneidio,
Ond am y ferch a welais ynddo.

49

Never was a girl so handsome,
Never was a girl so winsome,
Never did a girl come nearer
Breaking the heart of her true lover.

50

As I walked the beach this night
I saw a seagull, lily-white,
Gently upon the seashore wring
The soaking sea out of her wing.

I bowed my head, began to cry.
I found the seagull there close by.
'Under your wing, gull, carry far
This letter for my dear bright star.'

51

If I should ever lose my darling,
Flowers of the wood would lose their blooming,
And the birds would lose their mirth.
May God preserve the fruits of earth.

52

Handling those strings, that harp of gold,
Golden the harpkey in his hold —
Under his fingering, like those three,
Is where I wish my heart could be.

53

There is the grove that's set apart,
The green birch grove that breaks my heart:
For her, not for the grove, my grief is,
That girl I saw beneath its branches.

54

Maent yn dywedyd ar i fyny
Mai am y goch yr wy' 'n ymdynnu.
Minnau sydd ar dorri 'nghalon
Am y ferch â'r aeliau duon.

55

Rhois fy mryd ar garu glanddyn;
Fe roes hwn ei serch ar rywun;
Honno roes ei serch ar arall; —
Dyna dri yn caru'n anghall.

56

Dacw'r llwyn o fedw nwyfus;
Dacw seren y tair ynys;
Dacw fab â'r golwg tirion;
Dacw doriad llawer calon.

57

Ni cha' i siarad gair am gariad
Na fydd clustiau'r cloddiau'n clywad;
'Cawn i noswaith olau loergan,
Mi dorrwn glustiau'r cloddiau â chryman.

58

Nid oes rhyngof a'm gwir galon
Ond llwyn o goed a lled yr afon,
A drwg 'wyllys fy nghymdogion, —
Ofni'r wyf fod hynny'n ddigon.

59

Ni raid i'r ferch a gaffo Robin
Fynd â'r fules byth i'r felin,
Nac i gyrchu dŵr o'r afon;
Ar ei gruddiau hi gaiff ddigon.

54

They say about me there above
It's with the redhead I'm in love.
The truth is that my heart will break
For the black-browed beauty's sake.

55

I doted on a handsome boy.
Some other girl seemed all *his* joy,
And *she*, for certain, loved another.
Could foolishness in love go further?

56

There gay birches of the woodlands,
There the Star of these Three Islands,
There the gentle lad whose smiling
Means that many hearts are breaking.

57

I can't speak a word of loving
But the hedge's ears are listening.
One moonlight night, as bright as nickel,
I'll chop those ears off with my sickle!

58

Only between me and my lover
A clump of trees and width of river,
And my neighbours' spitefulness.
These will be enough, I guess.

59

The girl who marries Robin never
Need take the mule to mill or river
Fetching the water each one seeks.
She'll find plenty on her cheeks.

60

Dacw'r bedd 'r wy' 'n myned iddo,
Dacw'r wialen fesur arno,
Dacw'r arch a dacw'r amdo,
Os fy nghariad a'm try heibio.

61

Ow gan wylo, ow gan alar,
Ow na bawn i dan y ddaear,
Neu gael clywed gair oddi wrthi,
Sut y mae f'anwylyd arni.

62

'O f'anwylyd, prŷn im amdo
Prŷn im arch a dyro fi ynddo.
O f'anwylyd, cladd fi'n rhywle
Nes dêl d'wyneb tirion adre.'

'O f'anwylyd fwyn gysurus,
Paid â magu clwyf hiraethus;
Bydd di iach er gwaethaf undyn, —
Dof yn f'ôl cyn pen y flwyddyn.'

63

Tyn dy gleddyf gloyw gwisgi,
Tor fy mhen, maddeuaf iti.
Gwell yw gennyf hynny'n dawel
Na rhoi fy llaw i ganu ffarwel.

64

'R oeddwn hefo'r hwyr yn rhodio
Gerddi gwyrddion i'm comfforddio,
Uwch fy mhen clwyn fwyn lymysten,
Oer yw'r loes, beraidd foes yn uchel ochen.

60

There the grave that I must lie in,
There the yard-stick, there the coffin,
There the shroud — should she refuse
My death shall put all these to use.

61

Oh, I weep, and oh I grieve!
Oh, that I were in my grave!
Or hear that word to end these cares,
Telling me how my darling fares.

62

'Buy me a shroud, love, I must die;
Buy me a coffin, let me lie,
Sweetheart, in my burial place —
Till comes home your darling face.'

'Oh my sweetheart, do not nurse
That longing sickness, and its curse.
Be well, in spite of all you'll rest
Before the year's end, on my breast.'

63

With your bright sword strike off my head:
I shall forgive you — being dead
Seems better far than calmly raising
My hand to say goodbye at parting.

64

Through green gardens one fine evening,
For my comfort I went wandering,
Overhead a gentle falcon —
Cold the pain, sweet the wane of grief's abandon.

Nesu wnes yn ewyllysgar,
At fwyn ei llais a main ei llafar,
A than ufudd ofyn iddi,
'Er mwyn Duw, y fwyna' 'n fyw, beth yw dy g'ledi?'

Dyma'i hateb a'i hesgusion,
'Aml gnoc a dyr y galon,
Unig wyf ymysg yr adar,
A'm gado'n gaeth yma wnaeth fy nghymwys gymar.'

65

Ym Mhenybont ar ddydd y farchnad
    Cwrdd â'm cariad wnes yn brudd:
'Roedd hi'n prynu'i gwisg briodas
    Gyda deigryn ar ei grudd.

66

Mi rois fy lliw yn llawen
I Fadog dan y fedwen.
    Mi werthais i fy neurudd goch
    I'w rhoi i fochgoch fachgen.

67

Dy ddwy wefus, Besi bêr,
    Sydd iredd dyner aeron;
Ac mor felfededd, geinwedd, gu,
    Fel gweunydd blu dy ddwyfron.
On'd yw ryfedd, teg dy liw,
    Mor galed yw dy galon?

68

Mae'n dda 'mod i'n galed fy nghalon,
Lliw blodau drain gwynion yr allt;
Mae'n dda 'mod i'n ysgafn fy meddwl,
Lliw'r banadl melyn ei gwallt;

I made my way without avoidance
Towards her of the gentle utterance,
And I said, a grieving shadow,
'For God's sake, why this heart-break? What can be
    your sorrow?'

This is the answer I heard spoken,
'With many blows the heart is broken.
Amongst the wild birds I'm a prisoner —
Here alone, on my own, left by my darling lover.'

65

In Penybont on market day
    I met my sweetheart, pale and meek,
Buying with him, her wedding dress,
    A tear bright upon her cheek.

66

I gave my colour gladly
To Madog under the birch tree,
I sold my two red cheeks to him —
The red-cheeked lad that had me.

67

Your two lips, my pretty Bess,
    Are ripe as scarlet berries;
And smooth as cotton-grass, dear girl,
    The velvet of your breasties;
How is it that your heart is hard
    As rock of granite quarries?

68

I'm glad now that I am quite heartless,
    You, white as the thorn flowers fair;
I'm glad that I'm shallow and thoughtless,
    You, girl of the broom-yellow hair;

Mae'n dda 'mod i'n ieuanc, 'r wy' 'n gwybod,
  Heb arfer fawr drafod y byd;
Pam 'peidiaist ti, ferch, â'm priodi
  A minnau'n dy ganlyn di cyd?

69

Trwm yw fy nghalon a chlwyfus a chlaf
A phell yw fy nghariad; ow, ow, beth a wnaf?
Mae digon yn aros, nid wyf i ddim gwell;
Fy nghalon sy'n tynnu at hwnnw sy 'mhell.

70

Pe bawn i mor ddifalch â thywallt fy ngwaed
I gyd i ryw lestryn i olchi dy draed,
Drachefen eu sychu â gwallt fy mhen i,
Efallai'n y diwedd mai digio wnaet ti.

71

Dacw 'nghariad, mi 'i gwelaf o draw,
A gwasgod gron felen, a chwip yn ei law,
A lodes lân writgoch yn agos i'w glun,
Yn sôn am gariadau, — minnau heb 'r un.

72

F'anwylyd fain olau, pe gwyddit fy nghlwyf,
Ni fynnit fod undyn y modd ag yr wyf;
Mewn dolur difesur dyfeisia, fy mun,
Oes fodd it fy safio a'th gadw dy hun?

73

Genn't ti, fy mun eglur, i'm dolur, fain ael,
Mae pur feddyginiaeth, deg eneth, i'w gael.
'Does awr yn y diwrnod, lliw'r manod, i mi
Heb ddangos car'digrwydd net hylwydd i ti.

I'm glad that I'm young, without knowledge
   Of all the great world's right and wrong —
Why wouldn't you marry, my darling,
   This lad who has loved you so long?

69

How heavy my heart feels, how sick it is too;
My love has gone far off, Oh, what can I do?
Though many are left here, what comfort are they?
My heart is drawn always to him far away.

70

If, slavish, I poured in a pan my heart's blood,
And washed both your feet in that bright crimson flood,
And then with the hair of my head wiped them dry —
Perhaps even then I'd see scorn in your eye.

71

Not far off I see the young man I love stand
In his waistcoat of yellow, his whip in his hand,
Beside him some rosy-cheeked girl having fun
Discussing their lovers — and me without one.

72

My beautiful darling, if you knew but my wound
You wouldn't wish any a hurt so profound;
I'm deep in distress, can you think of some plan
To save both yourself and your suffering man?

73

You have, my sweet darling, my fine-browed, I'm sure,
For all that afflicts me, my sweetheart, the cure.
There never was, drift-white, one hour when I
Did not show you kindness — you know I don't lie.

Cariad Ffyddlon

74

Blodau'r flwyddyn yw f'anwylyd,
Ebrill, Mai, Mehefin, hefyd;
Llewyrch haul yn twnnu ar gysgod,
A gwenithen y genethod.

Main a chymwys fel y fedwen;
Berth ei llun fel hardd feillionen;
Teg ei gwawr fel bore hafddydd;
Hon yw nod holl glod y gwledydd.

75

Dy liw, dy lun, dy law, dy lygad,
Dy wedd deg, a'th ysgafn droediad,
Dy lais mwyn, a'th barabl tawel
A'm peryglodd am fy hoedel.

76

Dacw f'annwyl siriol seren,
Hon yw blodau plwyf Llangeinwen;
Dan ei throed ni phlyg y blewyn
Mwy na'r graig dan droed aderyn.

77

O f'anwylyd, dywed imi
P'le mae gwreiddyn ffynnon ffansi;
Ai yn dy gorff, ai yn dy galon,
Ai yn dy lân wynepryd tirion?

78

Dacw 'nghariad ar y bryn,
Rhosyn coch a rhosyn gwyn,
Rhosyn coch sy'n bwrw ei flodau,
Rhosyn gwyn yw 'nghariad innau.

True Love

74

The whole year's blossoms is my darling —
April, May, June, flowers blooming;
Bringing sun where shadows thicken,
The living wheat-grain of all women.

As the graceful birchtree slender,
Lovely as the flowers of clover,
Radiant as a summer's morning —
She's what every country's praising.

75

Your form in grace, your eyes in brightness,
Your hand, your hue, your step in lightness,
Your gentle voice to friend and stranger —
These have put my life in danger.

76

There's my love, Llangeinwen's star,
Her form is where all blossoms are;
No grass-blade bends beneath her stepping
More than the rock beneath the fledgling.

77

Oh, my darling, tell me truly,
Where is the root and fount of fancy?
Your heart? Your body? In the dance
Of beauty in your countenance?

78

My darling's there upon the height;
Rose of red and rose of white;
Red rose blooms and soon is blown;
White rose she I call my own.

79

Hardd yw gwên yr haul yn codi
Gyda choflaid o oleuni,
Hardd y nos yw gwenau'r lleuad,
Harddach ydyw grudd fy nghariad.

80

F'anwylyd oedd dy ddau lygedyn,
Gwn mai arian byw sydd ynddyn';
Yn dy ben y maent yn chwarae,
Fel y sêr ar noswaith olau.

81

O mor gynnes mynwes meinwen!
O mor fwyn yw llwyn meillionen!
O mor felys yw'r cusanau
Gyda serch a mwynion eiriau!

Gwen ei brest a gwen ei bronnau,
Gwen pob man, a choch ei gruddiau;
Gleision lygaid, teg ymadrodd,
Glendid hon yn llwyr a'm lladdodd.

82

Melys iawn yw llais aderyn
Fore haf ar ben y brigyn,
Ond melysach cael gan Gwenno
Eiriau heddwch wedi digio.

83

Saif y lloer â'i chlustiau i fyny
Yn ddistaw, pan fydd Gwen yn canu.
Wel, pa ryfedd fod ei chariad
Yn gwirioni yn sŵn ei chaniad?

79

Lovely the sun's smile at its rising,
Bringing its armful of bright shining;
Lovely the moon's smile in high heaven —
My darling's cheek is lovelier, even.

80

Two rays of light your eyes, my love;
Quick-silver's in the way they move;
In your face they sparkle bright
As stars do on a clear night.

81

Oh, so warm her breast, my lover!
Oh, so dear that grove of clover!
Oh, so sweet are all our kisses,
Her talk of love the speech of bliss is.

White her breasts, her bosom bright,
Cheeks of red but all else white;
Blue eyes, sweet speech, mark this friend
Whose loveliness has brought my end.

82

Sweet to hear beyond most words
The morning songs of singing birds;
Sweeter to hear my Gwenno's warm
Words of peace, after a storm.

83

The moon's ears stand erect, listening,
Silent, when my Gwen is singing.
No wonder, then, that in her presence
Her lover dotes on every cadence.

84

Gwyn fy myd na bawn yn walch
Neu ryw aderyn bychan balch,
Mi wnawn fy nyth yng nghwr y gwely
Lle mae Nansi Llwyd yn cysgu.

85

Afon Conwy'n llifo'n felyn
Mynd â choed y maes i'w chanlyn;
Ar ei gwaelod mi rof drithro
Cyn y trof fy nghariad heibio.

86

Tra bo Môn a môr o'i deutu,
Tra bo dŵr yn afon Conwy,
Tra bo Marl dan Graigydibyn,
Cadwaf galon bur i Rywun.

87

Moes dy law, cei law amdani;
Moes dy gred, cei gred, os mynni;
Moes dy feddwl addfwyn, tirion;
Yn eu lle cei gorff a chalon.

88

Llawn yw'r môr o swnd a chregyn,
Llawn yw'r wy o wyn a melyn,
Llawn yw'r coed o ddail a blodau,
Llawn o gariad merch wyf innau.

89

Câr y cybydd gwd ac arian,
A phwy sydd nas câr ei hunan?
Myfi sy'n caru merch yn anghall
Ac yn bychanu popeth arall.

84

Were I a lucky bird of prey
Or any proud bird, I'd away
And in that bed I'd build my nest
Where Nansi Llwyd lies down to rest.

85

The river Conway's yellow mud
Carries whole trees down in its flood;
I'll take three tumbles on its bed
Before I'll leave her I'm to wed.

86

As long as Conway is a river,
And Anglesey is set in water,
And Craigydibyn rests on marl —
I'll keep my heart pure for my girl.

87

Offer your hand — you shall have mine;
Your faith — I'll worship at that shrine;
Offer your mind, so meek and kindly —
In their place take heart and body.

88

Full the tide of sand and sea-shells,
Full of yellow and white are egg-shells,
Full of leaves and flowers the grove,
Full am I of my girl's love.

89

A miser loves his bag of pelf,
And who can fail to love himself?
I love a girl to wild distraction, ·
And to all else pay no attention.

90

Tra bo eglwys yn Llanelli,
A'r wennol fach yn hedeg drosti,
A thra bo gwyngalch ar ei thalcen,
Caraf i fy siriol seren.

91

Yfais atad, glas dy lygad,
Trwy bur serch a ffyddlon gariad;
Yfa dithau, dwyael feinion,
At y mwya' a gâr dy galon.

92

Mae dwy galon yn fy mynwes,
Un yn oer a'r llall yn gynnes;
Un yn gynnes am ei charu,
A'r llall yn oer rhag ofn ei cholli.

93

Dacw long yn hwylio'n hwylus
Heibio i'r trwyn ac at yr ynys.
Os fy nghariad i sydd ynddi,
Hwyliau sidan glas sydd arni.

94

Aelwyd serch sy rhwng fy nwyfron,
Tanwydd cariad ydyw'r galon;
A'r tân hwnnw byth ni dderfydd,
Tra parhao dim o'r tanwydd.

A ffyddlondeb yw'r meginau
Sydd yn chwythu'r tân i gynnau;
Â maint y gwres nid rhyfedd gweled
Y dŵr yn berwi dros fy llyged.

90

While Llanelli has a church,
While little swallows above it lurch,
While white-lime's on its gable wall —
My darling star shall be my all.

91

I drank to you, my blue-eyed darling,
In pure passion, faithful loving;
Drink, my fine-browed one, this toast —
'To him who loves your heart the most'.

92

In my breast two hearts I hold;
One is warm and one is cold;
Warm's the one with which I love her —
With the cold I dread to lose her.

93

There beyond that nose of headland
The ship sails on towards the island;
If my darling is aboard her
Blue silk sails I see upon her.

94

Between my breasts love's hearth is burning,
My heart's what serves there as love's kindling;
And those flames will not expire
While such fuel feeds the fire.

Faithfulness — the bellows blowing
Fire to flame from its first glowing;
With such warmth, it is no wonder
Water from my eyes boils over.

95

Pe bae gennyf lonaid crochan
O ragorol aur ac arian,
Hithau yn ei chrys a'i ffedog,
Hi gâi ran hyd at y geiniog.

96

'Rwyf yn hoffi sŵn y delyn
Gyda'i their-res dannau melyn,
Ac mae'r medd yn ddigon melys
Nes caf brofi mêl ei gwefus.

97

Yn lle papur rhof ddail gleision,
Yn lle inc rhof waed fy nghalon,
Yn lle cwyr i'w ddyfal selio,
Mi rof wallt fy mhen i'w rwymo.

98

Mi sgrifennaf lythyr eurad,
Mi'i danfonaf at fy nghariad,
Mi rof inc ar bapur tenau,
Ac a'i seliaf â chusanau.

99

Ar lan y môr mae carreg wastad,
Lle bûm yn siarad gair â'm cariad.
O amgylch hon mae teim yn tyfu
Ac ambell sprigyn o rosmari.

100

Mae gennyf gangen o rosmari
Ar ben y Penmaen-mawr yn tyfu;
Pan fydd f'anwylyd i'n mynd heibio,
Fe fydd y gangen yn blodeuo.

95

If I had a cauldron packed
With gold and silver, and she lacked
Everything but shift and apron —
With her I'd share all in that cauldron.

96

Sweet harp music's my delight,
Triple yellow strings tuned right;
And mead is sweet enough to sip
Till I can taste her honeyed lip.

97

For paper, green leaves and instead
Of ink, the blood my heart has shed;
Not with wax I'll seal this letter —
Hair of my head shall bind it better. .

98

I'll write golden words and send
A letter to my loving friend;
I'll place ink on fragile paper,
Kisses shall serve for wax and taper.

99

By the seashore a flat boulder;
I took my sweetheart there and told her.
Thyme and some sprigs of rosemary
Grow round that flat rock by the sea.

100

A branch of rosemary I own;
On Penmaen-mawr this branch has grown.
When my sweetheart passes by
The branch bursts out in blooms on high.

101

Paham mae'n rhaid i chwi mo'r digio
Am fod arall yn fy leicio?
Er bod gwynt yn ysgwyd brigyn,
Rhaid cael caib i godi'r gwreiddyn.

102

Fe geir cywarch ond cynilo,
Fe geir tir ond talu amdano,
Fe geir glendid ond ymofyn,
Ni cheir mwynder ond gan Rywun.

103

Lle bo'r cariad wiw mo'r ceisio
Cloi mo'r drws, a'i ddyfal folltio;
Lle bo'r 'wyllys fe dyr allan
Drwy'r clo dur a'r dderwen lydan.

104

Llawer gwaith, lliw'r eira gwyn,
    Y bûm i'n synfyfyrio,
P'un a wnawn ai digio 'nhad
    Ai troi fy nghariad heibio;
Gwell i mi yw digio 'nhad
    Na throi fy nghariad heibio.

105

Maent yn dwedyd na ddaw meinwen
    Led y frwynen gyda mi
Am fy mod i'n fachgen hagar,
    Wrth ei hawddgar wyneb hi.

Dyna gelwydd, gellwch goelio;
    Cefais ran o'i mwynder maith.
Fe ddaw'r seren i'm cysuro
    Sul a gŵyl a diwrnod gwaith.

101

Why darling beauty, why reprove me
Because another claims to love me?
Though wind can shake the branch's shoots
Mattocks alone will shift the roots.

102

You can have wealth if you start saving;
You can own land if you start buying;
Bought beauty, even, you can own —
Tenderness comes with Her alone.

103

When two swear their love will last,
Useless to bolt the door up fast;
A will like theirs it was that broke
Through bolts of steel and through thick oak.

104

Many times, my white as snow,
    This is what I've been thinking;
Shall I make my father cross
    Or finish with my darling?
I'd rather make my father cross
    Than finish with my darling.

105

That sweet girl, they say, will never,
    No, not a reed's breadth, walk with me
Since as a boy I'm rather ugly
    And all loveliness is she.

What a falsehood — for, believe me,
    I have known her gentle ways:
She's the Star who brings me comfort,
    Sundays, week-days, holidays.

106

Myfi sydd fachgen ifanc ffôl
  Yn byw yn ôl fy ffansi,
Myfi 'n bugeilio'r gwenith gwyn
  Ac arall yn ei fedi.

'R wy' 'n dewis dyfod ar dy ôl
  Bob dydd ar ôl ei gilydd.
Tithau sydd, anwylyd fach,
  Yn decach, wynnach beunydd.

107

Fel y cuddia'r llwyni gleision
Ddolennog grwydriad Cynon,
  Dymunwn innau lechu'r ferch
Enynnodd serch fy nghalon.

108

Mi gariaf rhwng fy mreichie
Gaerdydd ac Abertawe,
  A Chasnewydd ar fy mhen,
O serch at Gwen lliw'r blode.

109

Mae 'nghariad i eleni
Yn byw yn South Corneli,
  Yn fain ei gwest, yn nêt ei phleth,
Yn wynnach peth na'r lili.

110

Ni charaf y glwfer na chobler na chrydd
Na 'sgogyn o deiliwr nac eilun o wŷdd
Nac un o'r mân grefftwyr, sut bynnag y bo,
Ni charaf, ni cherais un llencyn ond go'.

106

I'm just a young and foolish lad,
    Whose life is glad and honest;
I am the one who tends white wheat —
    Others shall greet the harvest.

I choose to follow in your ways
    From morning to day's ending;
You are my sweetheart and my love,
    My whitest, loveliest darling.

107

Dense groves with greenness hiding
The loops of Cynon's gliding —
    So I would like to shelter one
Whom I have won for darling.

108

In my two arms I'd carry
All Cardiff, yes, and Swansea,
    And Newport, too, upon my head,
For love of red-cheeked Gwennie.

109

My girl this year is Gwennie
Who lives in South Cornelly;
    Her waist is slight, her plait is tight,
She's whiter than the lily.

110

I don't love the glover or cobbler at all,
Not to toolmaker, tailor or weaver in thrall,
Nor any small craftsman — I state it herewith,
I loved, and I love now, no lad but the smith.

111

Mae 'nghariad i'n Fenws, mae 'nghariad i'n fain,
Mae 'nghariad i'n dlysach na blodau y drain,
Fy 'nghariad yw'r lana' a'r wynna' 'n y sir,
Nid wyf yn ei chanmol ond dwedyd y gwir.

Wych eneth fach annwyl, sy'n lodes mor lân,
A'i gruddiau mor writgoch, ei dannedd mân mân,
A'i dau lygad siriol, a'i dwy ael fel gwawn, —
Fy nghalon a'i carai, pe gwyddwn y cawn.

112

Mae bechgyn Ceinewydd yn ddedwydd mewn ffair,
Yn cyrlio'u gwallt melyn yn nhaflod y gwair;
Ond cyrlient eu gorau a byddent yn ffri,
Rhyw fab o blwy' arall sydd orau gen i.

114

Da gan 'sgyfarnog gael egin mis Mai,
Da gan wiwer gael collen a chnau,
Da gan gwningen gael twll o flaen ci,
F'anwylyd fain olau sy'n orau gen i.

111

My darling's a Venus, the sweetest girl born;
My darling is whiter than blooms on the thorn;
My darling's the loveliest this county can show —
I don't at all praise her, I just say what's true.

Sweet darling, my sweetheart, the loveliest of girls,
Her cheeks are so rosy, her teeth like fine pearls;
Beneath her brows' gossamer bright her eyes shine —
My heart would adore her if once she were mine.

112

The chaps from New Quay, how they relish the fair;
They curl in their hay-lofts their long yellow hair;
Let them curl till they're curly and trim to a tee —
From some other parish the lad to suit me.

113

The hare loves the shoots that sprout up when it's May,
The squirrel the hazels he hides in his drey,
And I love my darling as, chased by the hound,
The rabbit loves seeing the hole in the ground!

Doethineb Cariad

114

Edrych ar y dorth, os gelli,
Sut y mae yn cael ei thorri;
Os yw hi fel dau gorn lleuad,
Paid â chymryd hon yn gariad.

115

Cyn bod yn ddedwydd rhaid i'r gŵr
Gau ei lygaid weithiau'n siŵr;
Ac weithiau'r wraig, os bydd yn gall
A gymer arni fod yn ddall.

116

Ar lan afon mae dau ebol
A dwy goeden o griafol;
A phan êl y rhain i siarad,
Cewch wybodaeth pwy yw 'nghariad.

117

Tebyg ydyw'r delyn dyner
I ferch wen a'i chnawd melysber;
Wrth ei theimlo mewn cyfrinach,
Fe ddaw honno'n fwynach, fwynach.

118

Mi briodais bwt o wreigan,
Nid yn fawr fel fi fy hunan.
Wrth ystyried yr hen eiria,
O'r holl ddrygau gorau'r lleia'.

Love's Wisdom

114

That girl you think you'd like to wed —
Watch how she cuts a loaf of bread.
If she carves out a moon's horns when
She cuts the slices — think again!

115

A happy husband will be wise
From time to time to close his eyes;
And a wife, instead of swearing,
Sometimes pretend she's hard of hearing.

116

On the river bank — two ponies;
Also there two mountain-ash trees.
When these start to chat together
You'll be told who is my lover!

117

The gentle harp is like a fresh
Young maiden, and her tender flesh;
What follows fingering her in secret
Is something sweeter and more dulcet.

118

I chose a girl small as an elf
To marry, not big like myself,
Recalling words of that wise saw —
'"Choose the least evil" be your law.'

119

Pan fo haul yn twnnu'n wresog
Mae cyweirio gwair meillionog;
Yn eich blodau, Gwen lliw'r eira,
Y mae orau i chwithau wra.

120

Mwyn, a mwyn, a mwyn yw merch,
A mwyn iawn lle rhoddo'i serch;
Lle rho merch ei serch yn gynta',
Dyna gariad byth nid oera.

121

Dwedwch imi p'run sydd ora,
Ai mab coch â'i groen fel eira
Ai un melyn hawddgar tirion
Neu'r un purddu glân ei galon?

Os bydd coch, fe fydd cythreulig,
Os bydd wyn, fe fydd gwenwynig,
Os bydd o'n felyn, fe fydd yn fedrus,
Dyn yn ddu'r wyf i'n ei ddewis.

122

Hir yw'r ffordd a maith yw'r mynydd
O Gwm Mawddwy i Drawsfynydd;
Ond lle bo 'wyllys mab i fyned,
Fe wêl y rhiw yn oriwaered.

123

Ber yw'r nos a buan derfydd,
Buan iawn y cân yr 'hedydd;
Lle bo dau yn caru'n ffyddlon,
Ni chânt hwy siarad hanner digon.

119

When Sun shines hot throughout the day
It's best to attend to clovered hay;
Snow-white Gwen, best pick your groom
When your beauty's in high bloom.

120

Gentle, gentle, is the maiden,
Gentle, where her love is given;
Where a maid's love is first told
Never shall that love grow cold.

121

'Who's the best man, tell me now,
The red-head with the skin like snow?
The gentle one with yellow hair?
Or the jet black — come on, declare?'

'If he's red, then he'll be devilish;
If white as snow — spiteful and selfish;
Yellow will do the best he can,
But black I'd choose to be my man.'

122

Long and steep is every hill-path
Between Cwm Mawddwy and Trawsfynydd;
To the young lover pressing onward
The steepest climb seems sloping downward.

123

Short the night and soon it's over;
Short is the skylark's singing hover;
Faithful lovers find each day
Too short for half they want to say.

124

Mynych iawn y bydd fy nghariad
Bryd a llais wrth drefn y lleuad;
A phan fyddo'r lloer yn llawngron,
Dyna'r pryd y bydd hi'n fodlon.

Pan fo'r tywydd yn wresogaidd,
Bydd fy meinir yn dra mwynaidd;
Pan fo'r hin yn oer aneiri',
Bydd fy seren wedi sorri.

Os oes coel ar bennau'r moelydd,
Buan daw yn chwerw dywydd;
Pan fo niwl ar Gadair Idris,
Yn ei thŷ ceir Lowri Lewis.

125

Tlws yw'r 'fallen ddyddiau C'lanmai,
Y mae oll yn ei llawn flodau.
Pan syrth y rhain, ni bydd gyn harddad;
Felly merch pan gollo'i chariad.

126

Pa waeth imi lodes wledig
Gyda'r nos na merch fonheddig?
Fe eill honno fod yn fwynach,
Ond bod crys y llall yn feinach.

127

Mi fûm gynt yn caru glanddyn,
Ac yn gwrthod pob dyn gwrthun;
Ond gweled yr ydwyf ar bob adeg
Mai sadia' 'r mur po garwa' 'r garreg.

Aros, mae y cerrig geirwon
Yn debyg iawn o fod yn freuon.
Carreg galed lefn a gwastad
Ddeil yn sadiach mewn adeilad.

124

Very often to the moon's phases
My love responds with different crazes;
When the full moon's round and radiant,
Then she's at her most compliant.

And, the weather at its warmest,
Then my darling feels her gentlest;
But the freezing cold of winter
Makes my star a sullen sulker.

If on the mountains omens gather,
Soon will come the bitter weather;
When there's mist on Cader Idris —
Look in her house for Lowri Lewis!

125

The apple tree it looks so handsome
On a May-day in full blossom —
Those blooms gone, it's not so charming;
So is a girl who's lost her darling.

126

What difference for me in the darkness —
Country girl or gentry mistress?
One may be tenderer but the other
Has the shift that feels the smoother.

127

'I loved a handsome boy like mad
Rejecting every common lad.
And yet the strongest masonry
Is built of roughest stones, I see.'

'Those rugged boulders — stop a little —
Prove quite often to be brittle,
And a stone wall, smooth and polished,
Is not so easily demolished.'

128

Ffals a choeglyd ydyw'r meibion,
Tyngu a gwenieithio'n greulon;
Gwneud i'r merched druain goelio
Peth na wnânt byth ei gywiro.

129

Geiriau mwyn gan fab a gefais,
Geiriau mwyn gan fab a glywais,
Geiriau mwyn sydd dda dros amser,
Ond y fath a siomodd lawer.

130

Ffôl wyf fi, a ffôl yw bagad;
Nid ffôl neb a gâr ei gariad.
Ffolach ydyw'r sawl a garo
Lle na bo ddim cariad iddo.

131

Pan fo gas gan hen gath lefrith,
Pan fo gas gan g'lomen wenith,
Pan fo gas gan alarch nofio,
Dyna'r pryd y dof i'ch ceisio.

132

Pwy na charai lanc o longwr
Sy'n troi mor ysgafn ar ei sawdwl,
A'i grys brith a'i necloth sidan,
A'i het Garléil a'i fyclau arian?

133

Rhaid i bawb newidio byd,
　　Fe ŵyr pob ehud anghall,
Pa waeth marw o gariad pur,
　　Na marw o ddolur arall?

128

All the boys are false and faithless,
Their flattery of poor girls shameless;
They pretend their love is plighted,
And do girls wrongs that can't be righted.

129

Sweet words from a lad I heard,
Sweet words by a lad were purred,
Sweet words came in great profusion.
Sweet words, sweet snare, sweet delusion!

130

I'm a fool — which isn't freakish.
Loving your girl though, that's not foolish.
The foolishness that's really grim
Is loving her who won't love him.

131

When the old cat treats milk with scorn,
When the pigeon loathes its corn,
When the swan hates swimming, then
I'll come to court you, sulky Gwen.

132

Who wouldn't love a sailor, turning
So neatly on his feet when dancing;
His Carlisle hat, his shirt all spotted,
His buckles silver, his silk scarf knotted!

133

That everyone must suffer change
     Is known to both dull and shallow;
What difference then to die of love
     Or of some other sorrow?

134

Er melyned gwallt ei phen,
Gwybydded Gwen lliw'r ewyn
    Fod llawer gwreiddyn chwerw'n yr ardd
Ac arno hardd flodeuyn.

135

Os collais i fy nghariad lân
    Mae brân i frân yn rhywle.
Wrth ei bodd y bo hi byw,
    Ac 'wyllys Duw i minne.

136

Mi fûm yn caru 'nghariad
    Am ddeuddeng mis ac un,
Gan feddwl yn fy nghalon
    Fy mod i'n eithaf un;
Yn lodes heini lawen
    Yn tyfu 'ngardd y byd, —
Nid oeddwn yn y diwedd
    Ond brechdan i aros pryd.

137

Nid cymwys dan un iau y tyn
    Ych glân ac asyn atgas;
Dwy natur groes mewn tŷ wrth dân
    Ni harddant lân briodas.

138

Mi glywais gan glywed, mi wyddwn fy hun,
Mai oer ac anghynnes yw caru hen ddyn.
Cynnig iddo gusan ac ato fo'n troi,
Na chawn gan yr henddyn na chymryd na rhoi.

134

However yellow shines Gwen's hair,
Foam fair — we know the venoms
  Of many bitter garden roots
Have lovely shoots and blossoms.

135

If I have seen my sweetheart go,
  Well, crow to crow's good riddance!
God grant her all crow's happiness,
  And me bless with his guidance!

136

I truly loved my sweetheart
  For more than one whole year,
My heart thinking he held me
  To be his only dear,
And I his happy sweetheart
  With a garden flower's appeal —
I was just bread and butter
  Sliced ready for his meal.

137

It isn't fair, I think, to yoke
  Fine ox and moke together;
For on one hearth two married minds
  Can make rough kinds of weather.

138

I know from experience, I've also been told,
It's comfortless loving an old man, and cold;
Offer him kisses, do all for his sake —
You'll get from an old man no give and no take.

139

Mae 'nghariad i 'leni yn byw yn Tŷ Fry,
A pherllan o 'fala wrth dalcen ei dŷ;
'R wy' 'n un o'i gariadau o bedair ar ddeg,
'R wy' 'n siŵr o gael afal cyn gynted â neb.

140

Cais lances a'th garo ped fai ond ei chrys,
A wypo dy feddwl pan godech dy fys.
Pe gwerit ti chweugain, ni ddywed hi air
Ond, 'Croeso, f'anwylyd; pa r' newydd o'r ffair?'

139

Up there in the Top House my sweetheart lives now,
And there in his orchard his apple-trees grow.
I'm *one* of his girls — he's got more than a couple! —
I'm as certain as anyone else of an apple!

140

Look out for a girl who may own but her shift,
But who knows what your will is at one finger's lift;
Who, if you spend ten bob, will not seem to care
But greet you with, 'Darling, what news from the fair?'

Natur a'r Tymhorau

141

Y sawl a dynno nyth y frân,
Fe gaiff fynd i uffern dân;
Y sawl a dynno nyth y dryw,
Ni chaiff weled wyneb Duw.

142

Mi fûm lawer bore difyr
A dechreunos yn fwy sicir,
Rhwng Penceint a Phlas Penmynydd
Yn gwrando ar fwynion bynciau'r 'hedydd.

143

Llawer gwaith bûm yn dyfalu
Lle mae'r adar bach yn cysgu,
Beth a gânt y nos i'w swper,
Pwy a'u dysgodd i ddweud eu pader.

144

Canmol deryn bach am ganu,
Canmol deryn bach am ddysgu,
Eto hyn sydd yn rhyfeddol —
Nid â deryn bach i'r ysgol.

145

Maent yn dwedyd am yr adar,
Nad oes un o'r rhain heb gymar;
Gwelais dderyn brith y fuches,
Heb un cymar na chymhares.

Nature and the Seasons

141

The one who robs the crow's nest shall
Burn in fire satanical;
The wren's nest-robber — his disgrace
Shall be to never see God's face.

142

Mornings I've been listening early
And at evenings just as surely,
Between Penceint and Plas Penmynydd —
To sweet lark-song, poured from sky's zenith.

143

Often I've seen the birds and wondered
Where the beds were where they slumbered;
At supper did they all have shares?
Who taught the little things their prayers?

144

We praise the little bird for singing,
We praise the little bird for learning;
The marvel is she has this knowledge
Though she's never been to college.

145

They say of birds it's their kind fate
That they shall never lack a mate.
I saw one once, sad and bespeckled,
By all the fierce flock's hate encircled.

146

Gwyn fy myd na fedrwn hedeg
Bryn a phant a goriwaered;
Mynnwn wybod er eu gwaethaf
P'le mae'r gog yn cysgu'r gaeaf.

Yn y coed y mae hi'n cysgu,
Yn yr eithin mae hi'n nythu;
Yn y llwyn tan ddail y bedw,
Dyna'r fan y bydd hi farw.

147

Fe ddaw Gŵyl Fair, fe ddaw Gŵyl Ddewi,
Fe ddaw'r hwyaden fach i ddodwy,
Fe ddaw'r haul fach i sychu'r llwybre,
Fe ddaw 'nghariadau innau 'n drwpe.

148

Mi godais heddiw'r bore,
Mi welais gywion gwydde,
    Egin haidd, ac ebol bach,
O, bellach fe ddaw C'lanme.

Llidiart newydd ar cae ceirch,
    A gollwng meirch o'r stable,
Cywion gwyddau, ebol bach,
    Pam na ddaw bellach G'lanme?

149

Mae'r gwcw wedi marw,
A'r boda rhwng y bedw,
    A'r adar mân yn fawr eu cân
Wrth weld y frân yn feddw.

146

'I wish that I could fly — I'd search
Hill and dale and never perch
Until I found out in what shelter
The cuckoo sleeps throughout the winter.'

'In the woods she takes her rest,
In the gorse she makes her nest,
Beneath the birch you'll see her lie,
For that's where she comes down to die.'

147

Soon comes St Mary's, St David's Day;
The little duck will start to lay,
The paths will dry out in the sun,
My girls will come in gangs for fun!

148

When I woke up this morning,
    I saw young geese out walking,
A new-born colt, some barley-shoots —
    Oh, now May-day is coming.

A new gate to the field of oats,
    The stallions leave their stables,
Goslings appear, a colt is born —
    When will May bring these marvels?

149

The cuckoo's dead, the dear,
The buzzard too, I fear;
    The little birds are in a funk —
The crow's blind drunk on beer.

150

Diofal yw'r aderyn,
Ni hau ni fed un gronyn;
   Heb ddim gofal yn y byd,
Ond canu hyd y flwyddyn.

Fe eistedd ar y gangen,
Gan edrych ar ei aden;
   Heb un geiniog yn ei god,
Yn llywio a bod yn llawen.

Fe fwyty'i swper heno,
Ni ŵyr ym mh'le mae'i ginio.
   Dyna'r modd y mae yn byw —
A gado i Dduw arlwyo.

151

Ar lan y môr heli ni thyfodd erioed
Na bedwen na gwernen na draenen ar droed,
Nac un math o goedydd ond llwyni o frwyn;
Dan gysgod y rheini daw defaid ag wyn.

152

Gwych ydyw'r dyffryn, y gwenith, a'r ŷd,
A mwyndir, a maenol, ac aml le clyd,
A llinos a'r eos ac adar a gân;
Ni cheir yn y mynydd ond mawnen a thân.

150

The little bird is much-blessed;
He doesn't sow or harvest;
 He has no care in all the world
But singing throughout the forest.

He sits among the branches,
He preens and never blenches
 Though there's no penny in his purse.
He's gay, though worse approaches.

Tonight he eats his supper;
Where will he get his dinner?
 That's the way he always lives —
On what God gives he'll prosper.

151

Beside the salt sea never grew a tree tall,
No birch tree, no alder, no thorn-bush at all;
No tree and no nothing but acres of rush —
That shelter serves ewes and their lambs for a bush.

152

The valley is lovely, the corn and the wheat,
The nooks and the pastures, the squire's retreat,
Nightingales, linnets — the birds sing in choirs.
All you get up the mountains is peat-bogs and fires.

Cariad Gorffwyll

153

Mynnaf brynu twca dima
I dorri twll yn nhroed yr Wyddfa,
Gael im weled Sir Feirionnydd,
Lle mae llunio pob llawenydd.

154

Sôn am godi pont o 'sglodion
Rhwng Sir Fôn a Sir Gaernarfon.
Gwallt fy mhen fydd ganllaw iddi,
Er mwyn y ferch sy'n tramwy trosti.

155

Anodd plethu dŵr yr afon
Mewn llwyn teg o fedw gleision;
Ond dau anos peth na hynny
Yw rhwystro dau fo'n ffyddlon garu.

156

Haws yw codi'r môr â llwy,
A'i roi oll mewn plisgyn wy,
Nag yw troi fy meddwl i,
Anwylyd fach, oddi wrthyt ti.

Haws yw malu'r graig yn llwch,
A'i rhoi oll mewn caead blwch,
Nag yw troi fy meddwl innau,
Anwylyd fwyn, oddi wrthyt tithau.

157

Mae fy nghariad wedi sorri,
Ni wn yn wir pa beth ddaeth ati.
Pan ddaw'r gwybed bach â chywion,
Gyrraf gyw i godi'i chalon.

Surrealist Love

153

A ha'penny knife I'll buy and cut
A spy-hole right through Snowdon's foot;
Then Merioneth sunshine I'll see,
The shaping place of gaiety.

154

They talk of building out of bits
A bridge across the Menai Straits.
For her sake who'll cross I'd dare
To plait a hand-rope from my hair.

155

It's hard to take the running rivers
Of green birch woods and plait their waters.
What's still harder is to keep apart
Two lovers, faithful, heart to heart.

156

Easier spoon the ocean up
And pour it in an eggshell cup
Than to turn my mind, it's true
My darling sweet, away from you.

Easier to grind the rocks to dust
And put them in a covered chest —
Easier this, my love, they'll find,
Than turning from you my true mind.

157

My girl has got the sulks, I see.
I can't tell what the cause may be.
When flies hatch their young again —
I'll cheer her with a fly's chick then.

158

Mi godwn y Gader ac ywen Llangywer
  I fynwent Llanaber, heb neb ond myfi;
Mi chwythwn dre'r Mwythig ar unwaith i'r Rennig,
  Ond siarad ychydig â Chadi.

158

I'd shift that old Cader, with the yew of Llangower,
 To Llanaber's graveyard, yes, no-one but me;
And Shrewsbury, Salop, I'd blow in a gallop,
 To speak to, I shall hope, my Cadi.

Gwatwaru Cariad

159

Mi rois goron am briodi,
Ni rof ffyrling byth ond hynny.
Mi rown lawer i ryw berson,
Pe cawn i'm traed a'm dwylo'n rhyddion.

160

Mi rois fy llaw mewn cwlwm dyrys,
Deliais fodrwy rhwng fy neufys,
Dwedais wers ar ôl y person,
Collais gwmni'r llanciau mwynion.

161

Mi rois fy llaw mewn cwmwl dyrys
Deliais fodrwy rhwng fy neufys;
Dywedais wers ar ôl person, —
Y mae'n edifar gan fy nghalon.

162

Gorau, gorau, gorau, gorau,
Cael y wraig yn denau, denau,
Ac yn ddrwg ei lliw a'i llun —
Mi gaf honno i mi fy hun.

163

Mi feddyliais ond priodi
Na chawn ddim ond dawnsio a chanu;
Ond beth a ges ar ôl priodi
Ond siglo'r crud a suo'r babi?

Siglo'r crud a'm troed wrth bobi,
Siglo'r crud a'm troed wrth olchi,
Siglo'r crud ym mhob hyswïaeth,
Siglo'r crud sy raid i famaeth.

Making Fun of Love

159

I paid five bob to marry Gwen.
I wouldn't pay five pence again,
I'd slip some parson fifty quid
If he could undo what he did.

160

My hand was in the noose's hold,
My fingers held the ring of gold,
After the priest, an oath I swore.
Now I shall see my mates no more.

161

In a thick cloud I thrust my hand,
Two fingers held a golden band,
And after Parson I said my part.
For this I'm sorry in my heart!

162

It's best to choose a wife that's skinny,
Her face in spots, hook-nosed and chinny,
Who's stood a good time on the shelf —
She's one I'll have all to myself!

163

I thought that once we'd had our wedding
We'd spend our time in song and dancing;
But since I'm married all I'm doing
Is sitting by the cradle, cooing,

Rocking it with my foot when baking,
Rocking it with my foot when washing,
Rocking it at my jobs like clockwork,
Rocking at all a mother's housework.

164

Tebyg ydyw morwyn serchog
I fachgen drwg mewn tŷ cymydog;
'A fynni fwyd?' 'Na fynnaf mono', —
Eto er hynny'n marw amdano.

165

Union natur fy mun odiaeth
Yw nacáu ymroi ar unwaith —
Gweiddi 'Heddwch', goddef teimlo,
Dwedyd 'Paid', a gadael iddo.

166

Tri pheth sydd yn anodd imi,
Cyfri'r sêr pan fo hi'n rhewi,
Rhoi fy llaw ar gwr y lleuad,
A gwybod meddwl f'annwyl gariad.

167

Ni wn i p'run sydd orau im eto,
Ai marw o gariad merch ai peidio,
Nes y gwypwyf pwy enillodd,
Ai'r mab a'i cadd ai'r mab a'i collodd.

168

Myn'd i'r ardd i dorri pwysi,
Pasio'r lafant, pasio'r lili,
Pasio'r pincs a'r rhosys cochion,
Torri pwysi o ddanadl poethion.

169

Mae gennyf gariad yn Llanuwchllyn
 dwy siaced a dau syrcyn,
A dwy het ar ei helw ei hun,
A dau wyneb dan bob un.

164

A sexy girl is like some boy
Who, in a neighbour's house, turns coy.
'Some food, son?' 'No, can't eat a bit.'
Yet longing for a meal of it!

165

The way my lovely's nature went
Was both to deny and give consent —
Allowing me, 'Oh, peace,' she cried
And saying 'Don't' would let things slide.

166

Three things that beat me all together —
Counting the stars in frosty weather,
Placing on the moon's edge my hand,
Figuring how Gwen's mind is planned.

167

I don't know if a man's best lot
Is to die of love or not
Until I see who's happiest —
The chap who won or he that lost.

168

Went to pluck a garden posy;
Passed the lavender and the lily;
Passed pinks and red roses too —
Plucked some nettles — all for you!

169

A Llanuwchllyn girl's my passion.
She's got two costumes, both in fashion,
Two matching hats as well, the peach,
And two faces under each.

170

Mae gennyf iâr a chlamp o geiliog,
Hefyd gywen felen gopog.
'R wyf mewn ffansi mawr i'th garu,
Pe cawn lonydd gan besychu.

Mae gennyf stwc, mae gennyf hidlydd,
Mae gennyf fuddai fechan newydd,
Mae gennyf ffansi mawr i'th garu,
Pe cawn i lonydd gan y diogi.

171

Mae gennyf gariad sydd yn fychan,
Mae yn methu cyrraedd cusan,
Y mae'n gweiddi am stôl i ddringo,
Yn fy myw ni chawn un iddo.

172

Mae f'anwylyd ar y ddaear
Wedi cael cynhaeaf cynnar,
Gwair heb ladd, yr ŷd heb fedi,
Ysgubor hefyd wedi'i llenwi.

173

Y mae bedwen yng Nghefn Traean,
Cainc yn aur a chainc yn arian.
Mae'n bryd iddi grino bellach,
Celodd lawer o gyfrinach.

174

Maent yn dwedyd ac yn dwndwr
Mae rhwng dwy y bûm i neithiwr.
Dyna wir na wiw mo'i wadu, —
'R oedd dwy gynfas ar y gwely.

170

'I've got a fine cock in my pen,
A tufted yellow chick, a hen.
I'd like to court you well enough —
If I could get rid of this cough.'

'I've got a strainer and a pail
I've got a new small churn as well.
I'd like to court you, I confess.
What holds *me* back is — laziness.'

171

I've got a lover who's so small
He fails to reach my lips at all,
And so starts shouting for a stool.
He'll get no stool from me, the fool.

172

It looks as though the girl I love best
Had this year an early harvest —
Hay not cut, and corn not reaping,
But the barn full up to bursting.

173

The Cefn Traean birch is old,
Branched with silver, branched with gold.
It's time it withered now — those boughs
Concealed too many of our vows.

174

There are rumours that I crept
Between two, late last night, and slept.
It's all quite true — all that is said —
There are two blankets on my bed.

175

Dau lanc ifanc aeth i garu,
Gyda'r afon ar i fyny,
Un â'i wn a'r llall â'i gledde, —
Cysgod bedwen 'trodd hwy adre.

176

Gwaetha' 'r gwynt yw chwythu,
Gwaetha' 'r glaw yw gwlychu,
    Gwaetha' 'r dydd yw dod i ben,
A gwaetha' Gwen fydd pallu.

177

Gwae fi erioed fy ngeni,
A 'nhad a'm mam fy magu,
    Na fuaswn farw ar laeth y fron
Cyn dod i oedran caru.

178

Peth ffein yw haul y bora,
Peth ffein yw blodau'r 'fala',
    Peth fein yw cariad fo gerllaw,—
Dyn helpo'r sawl fo bella'.

179

Os collais i 'nghariad oedd eneth fach lân,
Mi fedrai fyw hebddi, byw 'r oeddwn o'r bla'n.
Mi blannaf gyll crinion ar ochr y fron
I'r gog fach i ganu ei galar am hon.

180

Os collais fy nghariad ni chollais mo'm co',
Ni rwygaf mo'm dillad, beth bynnag a fo.
Mi godaf, mi gerddaf, mi fyddaf mor iach,
A chariaf fy ngalar ar ben fy mys bach.

175

Two bold lovers marched one evening
Up the hill to do their courting,
One with sword and one with gun —
The birch-tree's shadow made them run!

176

The worst of wind is blowing,
The worst of rain is wetting,
 The worst of day is that it ends,
The worst of Gwen's refusing.

177

Woe's me that they conceived me,
My Mam and Dad, and reared me;
 I wish I'd died upon the breast
Before love could molest me.

178

Lovely dawn sun that's radiant,
Lovely the bough that's fragrant,
 Lovely the sweetheart that lives near —
God help the dear that's distant.

179

If lost is the sweetheart I'd come to adore
I'll live now without her — I did it before;
I'll plant dried-up hazels along the hill-side
Where the cuckoo'll lament one who wasn't my bride.

180

If I did lose my sweetheart, I wouldn't go mad,
Nor tear up my clothes — I'm not that sort of lad.
I'll get up, I'll move on — now why should I linger? —
And I'll bear all my grief on my own little finger.

181

Mae 'nghalon gyn drymed amdani yn siŵr
Â'r bluen sy'n nofio ar wyneb y dŵr.
Fy serch a aeth ati a'm ffansi rhy ffôl.
Ni allaf gan chwerthin ddim wylo ar ei hôl.

181

I've lost her, my sweetheart, my heart for her sake
Is heavy as feathers afloat on the lake.
I fancied I loved her, my passion flew high,
I *do* shed some tears — I laugh till I cry!

Cariad Cas a Chenfigennus

182

Dacw 'nghariad i ar yr allt,
 chrib aur yn cribo'i gwallt;
A'th gariad dithau yn y cwm,
 chrib aur yn cribo'i mwng.

183

Dacw 'nghariad ar y dyffryn,
Llygad hwch a dannedd mochyn,
A dau droed fel gwadan arad',
Fel tylluan y mae hi'n siarad.

184

Mi af i'r eglwys ddydd Sul nesaf,
A than raff y gloch mi eisteddaf;
Ac mi edrycha' â chil fy llygad
Pwy sy'n edrych ar fy nghariad.

Love, Nasty and Jealous

182

My girl sits on the hill, she's fair
And with a gold comb combs her hair;
Down in the valley your girl
Combs out her mane without a curl.

183

That's my sweetheart there below,
Teeth of pig and eyes of sow,
Two feet based like ploughs for walking,
And a barn-owl's hoot for talking.

184

I'll go to church next Sunday morning
And sit there where the bell-rope's hanging.
Through my narrow lids, those men
I'll watch who've come to watch my Gwen.

Hwyl, Smaldod a Digrifwch

185

Onid rhyfedd, rhyfedd eilwaith,
Ydyw gweled gwŷr y gyfraith?
Maent yn ennill aur yn dyrrau
Gyda gweddol edyn gwyddau.

186

Maent yn dwedyd ac yn dwndwr
Mai'n y coed y bûm i neithiwr.
Dyna wir na wiw mo'i wadu, —
O goed i gyd y gwnaed y gwely.

187

Tri pheth a fedra' i orau —
Canu telyn heb ddim tannau,
Darllen papur gwyn yn groyw
A marchogaeth ceffyl marw.

188

Chwech o bethau a sych yn sydyn,
Carreg noeth a genau meddwyn,
Cawod Ebrill, tap heb gwrw,
Pwll yr haf a dagrau gwidw.

189

Af i gadw tŷ fy hunan,
Rhoddaf untroed ar y pentan,
A'r troed arall ar y pared,
Ac os llysg fy nghlun i, llosged.

Fun, Wit and Humour

185

I shall never cease to wonder
At the way the lawyers plunder;
Just a goose's quill — it's funny
How this makes them piles of money!

186

This latest rumour — is it right
That I was in the wood all night?
That you suspect is true, good folk —
My bedstead's made of solid oak.

187

Three things at which I'm pretty sharp —
Playing tunes on a stringless harp,
Reading off unprinted paper,
Putting a dead horse in a caper.

188

Six things soon as dry as chips —
Bare rock, and a boozer's lips,
April showers, tap without beer,
Summer puddles, the widow's tear.

189

Keeping house shall be my job;
I'll rest one foot upon the hob
And push the other up the wall.
I'll burn my legs? They'll burn, that's all!

190

Maent yn dwedyd bod yr wylan
Ar y traeth yn cadw tafarn,
Ac yn gwerthu'n rhad y ddiod, —
Dyna un o'r saith rhyfeddod.

191

Caseg winau, coesau gwynion,
Croenen denau, carnau duon,
Carnau duon, croenen denau,
Coesau gwyion, caseg winau.

192

Maent yn dwedyd yn Llanrhaead'
Mai rhyw deiliwr wnaeth y lleuad;
A'r rheswm am fod golau drwyddo
Ei fod heb orffen cael ei bwytho.

193

Tri pheth sydd yn Nant y Nantlle, —
Hen glos bwff Huw Wiliam Hwmffre,
A thas wair Siôn Robert Dafydd,
Llwdwn o geffyl Robin Gruffydd.

194

Dyn a aeth i ffair Cilgerran
A chanddo bwrs ac ynddo arian.
Yn y ffair, trwy ryw gamddeall,
Aeth y pwrs i boced arall.

195

Bûm yn claddu hen gydymaith,
A gododd yn fy mhen i ganwaith;
Ac 'r wy' 'n amau, er ei briddo,
Y cyfyd yn fy mhen i eto.

190

I'm told the seagull in some cavern
By the sea-shore keeps a tavern,
Where he sells cheap beer for fun.
Of the Seven Wonders — this is one!

191

Bay mare hack, your legs are whitish,
Black your hooves, your thin skin tightish;
Thinnish skin and hooves of black,
Long white legs, you old bay hack.

192

In Llanrhaeadr town one day,
A tailor made the moon, they say:
And this is why it lets in light —
The tailor didn't stitch it right.

193

Three things are in the Nant of Nantlle —
The old buff trousers of Huw Hwmffre,
The hayrick of Siôn Robert Dafydd,
The horse's colt of Robin Gruffydd.

194

A chap took to Cilgerran fair
His purse with money in, but there
It found itself, after some bother,
In the pocket of another!

195

A faithful friend of mine is dead
Who rose up often to my head;
And I don't doubt, although he's buried,
He'll rise again if I'm so minded.

196

Bûm yn caru ryw nos Wener
Dan y faril yn y seler,
Ac yn wir mi garwn eto
Gyfeillachu peth â honno.

197

Bachgen wyf o bridd a lludw,
Yfodd lawer iawn o gwrw.
Rhyfedd yw, wrth yfed lawer,
Nad âi'r pridd a'r cwrw'n forter.

198

Mi ddarllenais ddod yn rhywfodd
I'r byd hwn wyth ran ymadrodd,
Ac i'r gwragedd, mawr lles iddynt,
Fynd â saith o'r wythran rhyngddynt.

199

Ar y ffordd wrth fynd i Henllan
Cyfarfûm a bachgen bychan;
Ac wrth im ag ef ymgomio
Bachgen oedd a bechgyn iddo.

200

Tri pheth sy'n uchel ryfedd —
Cader Idris draw'n y Gogledd,
Pen Pumlumon, hynod fynydd,
A merch â het o'r ffasiwn newydd.

201

Tri pheth sydd yn hawdd eu siglo —
Llong ar fôr pan fo hi'n nofio,
Llidiart newydd ar glawdd cerrig,
Het ar gorun merch fonheddig.

196

One Friday night I went out courting.
In the pub cellar I was lying,
Under the barrel on the floor.
That sort of courting calls for more.

197

I'm a chap of earth and dust
Who's drunk his beer fit to bust;
It's strange I've not, with so much water
In all that booze, turned into mortar.

198

This is what I read — that each
Land's language has eight parts of speech;
Seems the women grabbed — God bless 'em —
Seven parts of the eight between them.

199

Going up Henllan road one day,
I met a small boy on the way.
We chatted, and I found this gnome
Had small boys of his own at home!

200

Three great marvels of this earth —
Cader Idris in the north,
The topmost summit of Plynlimon,
A girl whose hat's the latest fashion.

201

Three things that soon begin to rock —
A ship that feels the ocean's shock,
A gate set in a stony bed,
A hat perched on a posh girl's head.

202

Brith yw sêr ar noswaith olau,
Brith yw meillion Mai a blodau,
Brith yw dillad y merchedau,
A brith gywir ydynt hwythau.

203

Hen gath wen un lliw â'r lili
Oedd gan Owen Siôn a Lowri.
Daeth i hon farwolaeth greulon,
Aeth i rwyfo gyda'r afon.

204

Ci a chath a chyw a chywen
Yw cwmpeini Marged Owen.
Pan fo Marged Owen brudda'
Daw y rhain o'i blaen i chwara.

205

Tri pheth sy'n anghymesur,
Gwraig ysgweier ar ystrodur,
Dillad duon am ddyn pengoch,
A reiding-gown i'r wraig o Gwmcloch.

206

Gan y wraig sy 'Ngalltyfoty
Y mae peilliaid yn y gwely;
A dau glap o fenyn newydd
Sydd o dan yr hen obennydd.

207

Mae gan Marged fwyn ach Ifan
Glocsen fawr a chlocsen fechan,
Un i gicio'r cŵn o'r gornel,
A'r llall i gicio'r gŵr i gythrel.

202

Spotted with stars, each clear night;
Spotted with flowers, the May-day light;
Spotted are the girls' new dresses,
And spotted the girls themselves, my guess is.

203

White, as white as any lily,
Was the cat of Siôn and Lowri.
Cruel was the death fate gave her —
She went rowing down the river.

204

A dog, a cat, a chick, a chicken —
These are the friends of Marged Owen.
When the hours start to bore her
These come forth and play before her.

205

Three things beyond all computation —
The squire's wife in equitation,
A red-head in a suit of black,
Mrs Cwmcloch's riding tack.

206

Galltyfoty's wife, it's said,
Keeps sacks of flour in her bed!
And what are those big lumps of yellow?
New butter-pats beneath her pillow!

207

The clogs of Marged, Ifan's lass,
Large and small, are tipped with brass;
She kicks her dogs until they yell,
And her poor husband, all to hell.

Mae gan Marged fwyn ach Ifan
Delyn fawr a thelyn fechan;
Un i ganu yng Nghaernarfon,
A'r llall i gadw'r gŵr yn fodlon.

Ac mae ganddi, heblaw corlan,
Geffyl mawr a cheffyl bychan;
Un i gario'r gŵr o'r dafarn
A'r llall i gario'r god a'r arian.

208

Llances wen ofynnodd imi
Faint oedd rhwng y Pasg a'r Pandy;
Minnau atebais yn gymhennig,
'Fel i'r felin o'r Nadolig'.

209

Y sawl sy'n hoffi 'ngharu, cared;
Y sawl sy'n hoffi peidio, peidied.
Mae 'nghynhysgaeth yn fy mhoced,
Dimai goch, a dim ychwaneg.

210

Maent yn dwedyd i'ch balchïo
Eich bod yn lân, a chwithau'n coelio.
Gwn na chlywsoch chwi, ysgatfydd,
Yn eich oes ddim cymaint celwydd.

211

Codi'i chloch o hyd 'r oedd Sionad
Am ei bod hi heb 'r un cariad;
Ac yrŵan, wedi priodi,
Nid yw fymryn gwell nag oedd hi.

Marged, Ifan's girl, is sharp,
Playing her big and her table harp;
One's to pluck where singers meet —
The other keeps her husband sweet.

Marged has a horse that stands
(Besides a pony) fourteen hands;
Her husband, boozed up, likes small nags;
The big one bears her money-bags.

208

A girl asked (one of those leg-pullers),
'How far from Easter to the fuller's?'
I answered her with scolding skill —
'Like from Christmas to the mill!'

209

Those who love to love me, let them;
Those who don't love, I'll forget them.
My pocket holds my wealth in store —
One red ha'penny, nothing more!

210

To flatter you, they say you're pretty,
And you believe them, more's the pity.
I can tell you — truth will die
Before you hear a bigger lie.

211

Jane had no sweetheart, and this truth
Put a bell in her every tooth;
Now that she's married none rejoices,
For nothing silences her voices.

212

'Dacw 'nghariad yn mynd heibio,
A cheffyl glas ei feistr tano,
A'i ddwy law ar ben ei glun
Fel pe bae'n farch iddo'i hun.'

'Ni buasai raid it, ferch fonheddig,
Ddannod imi 'ngheffyl benthyg;
Maent yn dwedyd hyd y pentre
Y gallwn gael dy fenthyg dithe.'

213

Och a fi na lwfiai'r gyfraith
Im briodi dau ar unwaith;
'R wyf yn caru dau'r un enw,
Siôn ŵr ifanc, Siôn ŵr gweddw.

214

'R wyf yn caru dwy'r un enw,
Un yn lân a'r llall yn salw,
Gan y salw mae yr arian,
Ond gan y lân y mae y cusan.

215

Mae gennyf bedwar o gariada,
Af i'w gwerthu i ffair y Bala,
Un am ddim a'r llall am ddima,
A'r ddau eraill am geinioga.

216

Pe cawn weled dau gynhebrwng
Yr un dydd, rhown bunt o offrwm, —
Eich gŵr chwi, fy seren olau,
A'r wraig anynad sydd gen innau.

212

'That's my follower on the gray
His master's lent him for the day,
His arms akimbo, as though the horse
Belonged to him and not his boss.'

'There's no need to smirk, my lady,
Because I'm on a borrowed pony;
In the village, *and* it's true,
They say that I can borrow you.'

213

I wish the law allowed the crime
Of marrying two men at a time;
Two with one name I dote upon —
John the young man and widower John.

214

Two girls I love are both called Jane;
One Jane's pretty, one is plain;
Plain has money — how nice this is!
Pretty is the one for kisses!

215

Those four sweethearts that I've got —
In Bala fair I'd sell the lot;
One for nothing, one might reach
A ha'penny, two a penny each.

216

If two funerals in one day
I saw, I'd give a pound away —
Your husband's, bright star of my life,
And that peevish one's, my wife.

217

'Dywed imi, 'r ddwy ael feinion,
Pwy fu neithiwr yn dy ddanfon,
A'i law fain a'i faneg siefrel
Am dy fraich di'n pwyntio chwedel.'

'Pam mae'n rhaid i chwi'r mo'r holi,
Nac ychwaith i mi fynegi?
Ifanc wyf ac ansynhwyrol, —
F'ewyrth fu'n rhoi imi gyngor.'

218

Siôn fy mrawd a brynodd wn
    Am bumswllt crwn ar G'lame;
Wrth saethu targed ar das wair,
    Fe laddodd dair o'r gwydde.
Rhaid i bob ergyd, meddai coel,
    Fynd fel yr hoel i rywle.

219

Maent yn dywedyd fy mod i
    Yn caru Pegi'r Bwgan;
Ni fûm erioed ar lawr ei thŷ,
    Ar feddwl caru'r faedan;
Ac ni rois erioed mo'm serch
    Ar weflau merch mor aflan.

220

'R oedd gafr wrth droed yr Wyddfa
    Yn sownd wrth aerwy bren,
A bwch yn Ynys Enlli
    Yn bygwth taro pen.
Wrth sŵn y rhain yn taro,
    Yn ôl chwedel chwith,
Fe syrthiodd clochdy'r Bermo
    Na chodwyd mono byth.

217

'Answer, honest, brow of white —
Who was it brought you home last night,
His slender hand, in its kid glove,
Upon your arm, as though in love?'

'Such questioning I never heard!
I'm not obliged to say a word.
I'm young, I'm heedless — it was my nice
Uncle, who brought me good advice.'

218

John my brother bought a gun,
  And placed some bird-shot in it;
Aimed at the rick — a goose came by,
  He didn't mean to kill it.
Every bullet, the proverb says,
  Somewhere has its billet.

219

This is what they say, that I
  Go courting Bogy Betty!
I've never set foot in her house
  Thinking to court that nasty,
Nor ever laid the seal of love
  On lips that look so filthy!

220

There was a goat in Snowdon,
  Most fierce had he grown,
And a big buck in Bardsey
  Threatening to charge him down.
The sound of these two clashing,
  Or so say Barmouth men,
Made Barmouth's belfry topple,
  Never to rise again.

221

Yma'n gorwedd yn y clai
    Mae Modryb Siân o'r Hafod,
Yr hon yr wythfed dydd o Fai
Ddechreuodd ddal ei thafod.

222

Pe bae'r Wyddfa i gyd yn gaws,
    Fe fyddai'n haws cael enllyn,
A'r Foel Gaer yn fara gwyn,
    A'r Llyn yn gwrw melyn.

223

Mi feddyliodd deuliw'r can
    Fy mod amdani'n dyner;
Ond hi gamsyniodd ar ei cham,
    Gwell genni'i mam o'r hanner.

224

Llawen iawn y gallwn fod,
    Pe cawn i god ac arian,
A phot a phibell wrth y tân;
    A chwmni glân a diddan.
A mynd brynhawn 'r ôl codi'r gwlith
    I garu nith Huw Bifan.

225

Beth wneir â merch benchwiban?
Beth wneir â cheffyl bychan?
    Beth wneir â thaflod heb ddim gwair?
Beth wneir mewn ffair heb arian?

Wel, rhoi y ferch benchwiban
I werthu'r ceffyl bychan,
    A chadw'r dawlod nes dêl gwair,
A mynd i'r ffair â'r arian.

221

Here she lies beneath the clay
My Auntie Liz the Lung,
Who on the twenty first of May
Began to hold her tongue.

222

If Snowdon turned one lump of cheese,
We'd all get easier eating —
Moel Gaer would be a loaf of bread,
The Lake red beer for boozing.

223

Fine-flour-white was sure that I
Cast a hot eye upon her.
How could she make a boob that big? —
I rather dig her mother!

224

This would make a lovely jag —
A nice big bag of money,
Good pals, singing, pipe and pot
Beside some pub's hot chimney,
Then to court Hugh Bevan's niece,
A tender piece, believe me.

225

'What's to be done with Mari?
What with my pint-sized pony?
What with my hay-loft with no hay
And fair-day with no money?'

'Well, put that flighty Mari
To sell the dwarfish pony;
Wait till the hay-loft's full of hay
Then fair-day you'll have money.'

226

Mi eis i greigiau Eryri,
Mi holltais hwy'n dafelli,
   Mi wneis i'r llwynog fod mor ffôl
Â theithio ar ôl milgi.

227

Mi welais ferch yn godro
A menyg am ei dwylo,
   Hidlo'r llaeth drwy glust ei chap,
A merch Sion Cnap oedd honno.

228

On'd ydyw yn rhyfeddod
Bod dannedd merch yn darfod?
   Ond tra bo yn ei genau chwyth,
Ni derfydd byth ei thafod.

229

Peth ffein yw llaeth a syfi,
Peth ffein yw siwgwr candi,
   Peth ffein yw myned wedi nos
I stafell dlos i garu.

230

Gwae fi na bawn yn gwybod
Am ffordd, heb ddod yn briod,
   I gael y canpunt sydd yn stôr
Gan ferch yn ochor Llwytco'd.

231

Mae'r frech ar wyneb Martha,
'R un faint â chwecheinioga,
   Er colli dau o'i dannedd bla'n,
Mae eto'n lân ei gwala.

226

On Snowdon's top how nice is
Cutting the rocks in slices,
  And setting the fox to chase the dog
Across the bog for prizes.

227

I saw a girl go milking
With gloves on — I'm not kidding!
  To strain the milk she used her cap —
Sion Cnap's girl I'm describing!

228

Now isn't it offending
A girl's teeth have an ending,
  But that her tongue, while she has breath —
Till death — will want no mending?

229

Wild strawberries are dandy,
And so is sugar candy,
  And chatting up your bird some night
You're fighting fit and randy.

230

I wish I knew some method,
Without the marriage period,
  Of getting that one hundred quid
Owned by that kid from Llwytco'd!

231

Though Martha looks small-poxy,
Her sixpenny scars are sexy;
  And though she's lost her two front teeth
She's still a pretty doxy.

232

Pe bai taranau'n rhuo a hefyd gloch y llan,
A rhod y felin bapur a gyrdd y felin ban,
A'r badell bres a'r crochan yn tymblo draws y tŷ,
A phawb yn gweiddi yma, cysgu a wnâi hi.

233

Mae gennyf ddafad gorniog ac arni bwys o wlân,
Yn pori yng nglan yr afon, ymlith y cerrig mân;
Fe ddaeth rhyw hogyn heibio a hysiodd iddi gi,
Ni welais byth mo'm dafad: os gwn i a welsoch chwi?

Mi'i gwelais hi yn y Bala newydd werthu'i gwlân,
A phibell a thybaco, wrth danllwyth mawr o dân.
O dwedwch wrth fy nafad am ddŵad at Siân Ddu;
Ni welais byth mo'm dafad: ai tybed welsoch chwi?

234

Llo bolgoch, llo cefnwyn, llo tirion, llo torwyn,
Llo hwylus, llo melyn, llo bronwyn yw hwn;
Llo main a llo mwynedd, llo llon a llo lluniedd,
Llo hoywedd diwaeledd, da welwn.

235

'Arhoswch, arhoswch, fy annwyl hen ffrind,
O peidiwch â digio. I b'le'r ych yn mynd?
Yn wrol ac addas atebodd y dyn,
'Af adref i yfed fy mhotes fy hun'.

236

Os daw yr hen Ffrancod fel buont o'r blaen
I ymladd â Lloegr, na hitiwch mo'r draen.
Ni wnânt hwy ddim niwed i ni, 'neno'r tad,
Tra bydd Dafydd Ifan a'i wn yn y wlad.

232

The thunder can be deafening, the church bells
    tolling loud,
The paper mill and flour mill both roaring like a crowd,
The pitcher and brass cauldron can tumble through
    the house
And all of us start bawling — she'd still sleep like a mouse!

233

'She grazes by the river, my dear horned sheep, and bears
A heavy load upon her — the thick wool fleece she wears.
But now some rascal's got her, although I don't know who.
Do you happen to have seen her? Please tell me if you do.'

'I saw her up in Bala, where she'd just sold her fleece,
Sitting by the fire, smoking her pipe in peace.'
'If you should see that horned one, please send her
    home to me.
Oh, to set eyes upon her! Oh, where *can* she be?'

234

One calf is red-bellied and white-backed and gentle,
And this one is yellow and gay, as you see;
Another is slim and pale-chested and handsome,
And happy and noble and shapely.

235

'Oh, hear me, please wait, I don't mean to offend!
Wait — where are you hurrying to, dear old friend?'
He answered me coolly, quite calm, without wrath,
'I'm on my way home to drink up my own broth!'

236

Now if those old Frenchmen again leave their patch,
And come to fight England, we won't care a scratch;
They can't do us harm, and God knows we won't run,
While brave Dafydd Ifan's abroad with his gun!

237

Glân fel y g'lomen ar nen ucha' 'r to
Yw morwyn gŵr gweddw, pan êl i roi tro;
Ond coeliwch neu beidiwch, y gwir a saif byth,
Mae hi'n slwt rwdi fudur yng nghanol ei nyth.

238

Mae 'nghariad i 'leni yn byw gyda'i fam,
A'i ysgwydd yn grwca a'i gefen yn gam;
Ac ymladd â'r cathod bob diwrnod y bydd.
Yr wyf yn ei garu er hynny'n o rydd.

239

Fan yma y gorwedd corff Ifan Siôn Crwn,
Fe hedodd ei enaid i rywle na wn;
Os cas ef drugaredd, trugaredd sy'n bod,
Gan na wnaeth drugaredd ag undyn erio'd.

240

Difyr yw hwyaid yn nofio ar y llyn,
Eu pigau sy'n cochion a'u plu sydd yn wyn.
Rhônt ddeudro neu drithro yn fywiog a chwim.
Beth bynnag welant, ni ddwedant hwy ddim.

241

Bu farw cath modryb, bu farw cath Gwen,
Bu farw'n cath ninnau gan gur yn ei phen;
Mae cath y drws nesaf yn glaf o'r un clwy';
Mae mall wedi dyfod ar gathod y plwy'.

237

The widower's servant, out walking, aloof,
Is neat and as clean as the dove on the roof.
Believe me, believe me not, the truth is the best,
She's a filthy young slut when she's home on her nest.

238

My sweetheart at present lives home with his Mammy;
His shoulders are crooked, his back has grown gammy;
He fights with the cats every day of his life —
I hope all the same that I'll soon be his wife.

239

Here lies the body of bent Evan John.
We know his soul's left him — but where has it gone?
If *his* soul has mercy, then mercy's for all —
He showed no-one mercy, no mercy at all.

240

How pretty to watch are the ducks and their drake,
Red-beaked and white-feathered, afloat on the lake;
They tip up their bottoms — whatever they've heard,
Whatever they've seen then, they don't say a word.

241

Gwen's tom-cat has passed on, our Auntie's is dead;
And our cat died with a pain in his head;
The cat from next door's looking no more than fairish —
There must be a plague on each puss in the parish.

Profiad a Doethineb

242

Da am dda sy dra rhesymol,
Drwg am ddrwg sydd anghristnogol,
Drwg am dda sydd yn gythreulig,
Da am ddrwg sy fendigedig.

243

Lle bo cariad fe ganmolir
Mwy, ond odid, nag a ddylir;
A chenfigen a wêl feiau
Lle ni bydd dim achos, weithiau.

244

Pan fo seren yn rhagori,
Fe fydd pawb â'i olwg arni;
Pan ddêl unwaith gwmwl drosti,
Ni fydd mwy o sôn amdani.

245

Ofer ydyw saethu seren,
Ofer golchi traed hwyaden;
Ofer ydyw, cofia'r ddameg,
Iro tor yr hwch â bloneg.

Ofer ceisio grawnwin deall
Ar fwyeri, drain, ac ysgall;
Ofer disgwyl y felgafod
Yn ddefnynnau ar y wermod.

Ofer, ffôl yw'r dyn sy'n tybied
Ei fod heb farn yn medru cerdded;
Ni chariodd ci erioed ei gynffon
Wrth fodd pawb, mae'n hysbys ddigon.

Experience and Wisdom

242

Good for good is only fair;
Bad for bad soon brings despair;
Bad for good is vile and base;
Good for bad shows forth God's grace.

243

Love will give praise, I have observed,
Even where no praise is deserved,
And jealousy, alas, exalts
Small failings into mortal faults.

244

People point and marvel nightly
When a planet's shining brightly.
But should a cloud once hide its radiance
They soon forget the former brilliance.

245

Useless shooting at a star;
Washing ducks' feet won't get you far;
Recall the proverb — rubbing fat
On the sow's belly — what good's that?

Useless to expect the grape
On thorns or thistles to take shape;
Useless to search — the honey-dew
Never on the wormwood grew.

Useless, that man who thinks that none
Will ever question what he's done;
People's views are even varied
On the way the dog's tail's carried!

246

Hawdd yw dwedyd, 'Dacw'r Wyddfa,' —
Nid eir trosti ond yn ara';
Hawdd i'r iach, a fo'n ddiddolur,
Beri i'r afiach gymryd cysur.

247

Medi gwenith yn yr egin
Yw priodi glas fachgennyn;
Wedi ei hau, ei gau, a'i gadw,
Dichon droi'n gynhaeaf garw.

248

Esmwyth tlodi gan y doethion,
Blin yw cyfoeth i'r ynfydion.
Mwy o boen sy ar rai yn gwario
Nag ar eraill yn llafurio.

249

Pwy a gariai faich o gwrw
Yn ei fol i fod yn feddw?
Trymaf baich yw hyn o'r beichiau,
A baich ydyw o bechodau.

Hwn yw mam y cam a'r celwydd,
Lladd, a lladrad, ac anlladrwydd;
Gwna gryf yn wan, a gwan yn wannach,
Y ffel yn ffôl, a ffôl yn ffolach.

250

Mae cyn amled yn y farchnad
Groen yr oen â chroen y ddafad,
A chyn amled yn y llan
Gladdu'r ferch â chladdu'r fam.

246

Easy enough to say, 'There's Snowdon'.
Crossing it makes the toughest weaken.
Easy for those not suffering pain
To urge the sick not to complain.

247

Reaping wheat-shoots in the spring —
That's a young lad marrying;
Sow and mow and keep — his harvest
Will be garnered in the tempest.

248

Poverty for wise men's easy;
Wealth is a problem for the silly;
Some find spending far more painful
Than others labour when it's fruitful.

249

Who'd carry in his belly, drunk,
The load of beer that he'd sunk,
Since no heavier's borne within
Than this, which is a load of sin.

Drink — mother of untruthfulness,
Of murder, theft, and wantonness,
Makes the strong weak and the weak weaker,
The brainy dull, the dull still duller.

250

In the market one can see
Sheepskin and lambskin equally,
And in the churchyard watch the daughter's
Funeral as often as the mother's.

251

Mi wn am ferch yn Sir Forgannwg,
Yn deg ei thwf, yn hardd ei golwg,
A gwallt modrwyog, bronnau gwynion,
A düwch uffern yn ei chalon.

252

Tebyg iawn i'r môr yw'r merchad,
Weithiau'n mynd ac weithiau'n dŵad.
Pan fo'n dawel yn y dyfnddwr,
Ar y lan gyfyd cynnwr'.

253

Perchen tafod a arfero
Ddweud am bawb y peth a fynno,
Bydd rhaid iddo wrando'n fynych
Lawer peth na bo'n ei chwennych.

254

Amser sydd i dewi ar bopeth,
Amser sydd i ddwedyd rhywbeth,
Ond ni ellir cael un amser
I ddweud popeth yn ddibryder.

255

Bûm edifar fil o weithiau,
Am lefaru gormod geiriau;
Ond ni bu gymaint o helyntion
O lefaru llai na digon.

256

Gochel fostio'n fynych, fynych,
Y gweithredoedd gorau feddych,
Rhag cael dannod it yn rhydost
Y gweithredoedd gwaetha' wnaethost.

251

A girl lives in Glamorganshire
Whose beauty brings all men to her;
White breasts, curled hair, sleek and smart —
And all hell's blackness in her heart.

252

Girls are like the tides of ocean,
In and out in endless motion.
When their depths are still and silent
On their beach is endless movement.

253

The owner of a tongue that boldly
Says what he thinks of all and sundry,
Himself will often, to be truthful,
Hear many an unwelcome mouthful.

254

There's a time for saying nothing;
There's a time for saying something;
There never is a time for pouring
The whole truth out and never caring.

255

That I've repented often is good
For saying far more than I should.
I've had less trouble with the thought
I've sometimes said less than I ought.

256

Be careful that you do not boast
Of those good deeds you prize the most,
In case some cruel voice should taunt you
With all those dirty tricks that haunt you.

257

Clywais siarad, clywais ddwndro,
Clywais bart o'r byd yn beio,
'Chlywais i eto neb yn datgan
Fawr o'i hynod feiau'i hunan.

258

Ni chawn aros mwy na'n tadau, —
Awn i'r ffordd yr aethant hwythau,
Rhaid yw mynd i wneuthur cyfri',
Er mwyn rhoi lle i eraill godi.

Ni cheir gweled mwy o'n hôl
Nag ôl neidr ar y ddôl,
Neu ôl llong aeth dros y tonnau,
Neu ôl saeth mewn awyr denau.

259

Bûm yn byw yn gynnil, gynnil,
Aeth un ddafad imi'n ddwyfil;
Bûm yn byw yn afrad, afrad,
Aeth y ddwyfil yn un ddafad.

260

Geneth wyf sydd ar y dibyn,
Gerddodd lawer llwybr anhydyn;
Ac er hawsed i mi dripio,
Mi rof fy nhroed ar wastad eto.

261

Maent yn dwedyd y ffordd yma
Nad oes dim mor oer â'r eira;
Rhois ychydig yn fy mynwes,
Clywn yr eira gwyn yn gynnes.

257

I hear them all denounce and haver,
Scolding, blaming, all that palaver;
I've never heard one shouting loud
His own great failings to the crowd.

258

We shan't stay here more than others,
But go the way that went our fathers;
Having fulfilled our obligations
Give place to rising generations.

There's nothing of us but shall pass
Like the snake's track in meadow grass,
Or the ship's wake upon the ocean,
Or through bright air the arrow's motion.

259

When my life was thrifty, thrifty,
Soon my one sheep grew to fifty;
After that I lived for fun
And found my flock was back to one.

260

I am a girl upon the brink.
I've trodden worse paths, though, I think.
Although I seem about to fall
I'll tread the flat-lands after all.

261

This is what they say, I know,
That nothing is so cold as snow.
When I put this to the test
White snow seemed warm upon my breast.

262

Bu gennyf ffrind a cheiniog hefyd,
Ac i'm ffrind mi roes ei benthyg.
Pan eis i nôl fy ngheiniog adre,
Collais i fy ffrind a hithe.

263

Ac yr awron, 'r ydwy' 'n dechrau
Dallt y byd a chyfri' 'nghardiau,
Ac adnabod fy nghymdogion:
Duw, pa hyd y bûm i'n wirion?

264

Myfi ni charaf neb o'r aerod
Sydd â'u tir ar flaen eu tafod,
Ac yn disgwyl i'w tad farw;
Gwell yw hwsmon da na hwnnw.

265

Rhodio'r coed erioed yr oeddwn,
A chael dewis pren a fynnwn,
Fe ddewisais fonyn draenen
Yr lle llithrig lathraid onnen.

266

Os af dros y hiniog allan,
Daw fy ngwraig, un ddull â Satan,
Gan fy ngalw'n bob drwg enw
Hyllaf sydd gan fintai'r cwrw.

Codi'n fore at fy ngorchwyl,
Bywiol agwedd ar bob egwyl,
Ac er hyn mae'r wraig yn rhincian
Ers hir oriau eisiau'r arian.

262

I had a friend. He had no money,
So I lent this friend my penny.
When I asked back what was my own
I lost my friend and lost my loan.

263

I examine in my hand
My cards at last, and understand
How false my neighbours are, and mean.
God, what a simpleton I've been.

264

I never like as friends that gang
Whose land is always on their tongue,
Hoping for their father's end.
I'd sooner a servant were my friend.

265

Searching through the woods I wandered;
Which tree should I choose, I wondered.
I picked a prickly thorn, being rash,
And not a smooth and polished ash.

266

Before I step out from the house
My devilish wife begins her grouse
Against me — all that greed can utter
In the language of the gutter.

Rising early for my work,
Because, indeed, I never shirk,
Still I hear the wife's teeth gnash,
Pestering me for yet more cash!

Duw ro ras i ferched blinion
Sydd yn awdurdodi dynion,
Fel y caffont yn eu cyfnod
Fod yn glust ac nid yn dafod.

267

Canu wnaf a bod yn llawen,
Fel y gog ar frig y gangen;
A pheth bynnag ddaw i'm blino,
Canu wnaf a gadael iddo.

268

Duw, dy dlysed! Duw, dy laned!
O na châi fy mam dy weled.
A phe doit ti gyda mi adre,
Ti gait groeso os cawn inne.

269

Henffych well, fy hen gyfeillion,
O Fôn ac Arfon ac ym Meirion,
Lle mae sŵn a suo tannau,
Yn eich mwynder cofiwch finnau.

Yn eich cwmni mi fûm lawen,
Yn eich plith mi fûm ben-hoeden.
Ni feddyliais o feddalwch
Y dôi diwedd ar ddifyrrwch.

Dyddiau f'ienctid a'm bwytasant,
Rhwng fy mysedd diangasant;
Gwedi bwrw 'mlodau gwynion
Dacw'r ffrwyth yn blant ac wyrion.

Fe ddaw'r rhain 'r un modd â minnau,
Rhai'n dwyn dail a rhai'n dwyn blodau,
Rhai'n dwyn ffrwyth hyd ddiwedd amser, —
Ni wnaeth Duw un peth yn ofer.

God give grace to grasping wives
Who try to rule their husbands' lives
With grumbles, and demands, and jeers.
May they become, not tongues, but ears!

267

Always I'll be happy and sing
Like the cuckoo on the wing;
Troubles shall leave me as I am —
I'll sing and never give a damn.

268

God, you're lovely. God, you're sweet.
I long for you and Mam to meet.
If you'd visit her you'd see
You're welcome just as much as me.

269

I hail you, friends — your old companion —
In Môn, in Meirion, and in Arfon;
Where there are harps and revelry,
Of your kindness, think of me.

In your company was pleasure,
With you I seemed a different creature.
One thing I never comprehended —
Some day our joy would all be ended.

Youth ate me up from day to day,
Between my hands youth slipped away.
Behold now, life's white flowers fallen,
My fruits — my children and grandchildren.

As I did, these shall show their powers,
Some bringing leaves, some bringing flowers,
Some benefits to last for ever.
God shall not work in vain, no, never.

270

Bûm yn y Llan y Sul diweddaf,
A'm gown sidan oedd amdanaf,
Ac ebe'r merched wrth ei gilydd, —
'Dacw gariad Huw'r Melinydd'.

Os melinydd 'r wy' 'n i garu,
Siwgwr gwyn a fynna' i falu,
A rhoi llefrith i droi'r felin, —
Pwy fydd gwell na minnau wedyn?

271

Mam-yng-nghyfraith tu hwnt i'r afon
Yn gweld fy nillad yn rhy wynion;
'R oedd yn tybio yn ei chalon
Mai ei mab a roes y sebon.

272

Anodd cael, mae hynny'n eglur,
Gosyn glân o gawsellt budur.
Anodd felly fod gan Megan
Blant yn lân a hithau'n aflan.

273

Mae fy nghariad yn fy ngwrthod
Am na bawn yn berchen buchod;
Ond pe bawn yn berchen llo,
Ni chymerwn mono fo.

274

Betw fach yn gyrru i'r ffair
Ar ei march a'i chyfrwy aur;
Yntau Guto'r cwrcwd llwyd
Yn y lludw'n crio am fwyd.

270

As last Sunday I sat down
In church, dressed in my satin gown,
I heard the women round me whisper,
'That's the girl of Hugh the Miller'.

If I am a miller's lover,
What I shall wish to grind's white sugar
With buttermilk to turn the wheel.
I'd have no betters then, I feel.

271

Mother-in-law across the brook,
You give my washing many a look,
And think, since it's so white, the one
Who rubbed the soap in was your son.

272

It's hard to get — that's clear, I guess —
A clean cheese from a dirty press.
Why doesn't Meg observe this pattern?
Her kids are clean but she's a slattern.

273

How cool my follower's loving grows
Because I don't own any cows.
But even if I owned a calf
He'd never be my better half.

274

Dear Bet rides down to the fair,
A golden saddle on her mare;
Crippled Guto from his bed
In the gutter cries for bread.

270

'Lodes ei mam a lodes ei thad,
A fentri di gyda mi allan o'r wlad,
Lle mae'r gwin yn troi meline,
A chan punt am gysgu'r bore?'

'Na wrando mabiaith gweniaith gwad
Gwell im aros yn fy ngwlad,
Lle mae'r dwfr yn troi meline
A chlod fawr am godi'r bore.'

271

'R wyf yn ddall, yr wyf yn gweled,
'R wyf yn fyddar, 'r wyf yn clywed,
'R wyf yn glaf ac yn fy iechyd,
'R wyf yn fyw, yn farw hefyd.

272

Os bydd annwyd ar y mab,
Rhowch amdano gob ei dad.
Os anwydol fydd lliw'r can,
Rhowch amdani bais ei mam.

273

Duw a helpo'r morwyr druan,
Weithiau'n brudd ac weithiau'n llawan,
Weithiau aur ac arian ddigon,
Weithiau'n brin o ddŵr yr afon.

274

Pan basio gŵr ei ddeugain oed,
Er bod fel coed yn deilio,
Fe fydd sŵn 'goriadau'r bedd
Yn peri i'w wedd newidio.

270

You, daughter of your Mam and Dad,
Now will you risk it with this lad,
And come where mills are turned by wine
And to earn pounds you sleep till nine?

'I don't listen to such rubbish.
I'll stay on here, in my own parish,
Where mill-wheels still are turned by water,
Praised as an early rising daughter!'

271

I am blind but good at seeing;
Deaf as well, but with keen hearing;
I am sick, my health is fine;
I am alive — death too is mine.

272

If a bad cold's troubling Jack,
Put his Dad's coat upon his back;
If it troubles daughter Jill,
Mam's petticoat will cure the chill.

273

May God have mercy on poor seamen,
Sometimes glum, now gay as gleemen;
Sometimes rich in gold and silver
Sometimes lacking drinking water.

274

When a man's turned forty, though
   His outward show is brave,
One sound will wipe his smile away —
   The digging of a grave.

275

Yn y 'sgubor efo 'nhad
    Y bu rhyw siarad digri';
Fe wnaeth arna' i lygad cam
    Pan soniais i am briodi.

276

Yma a thraw y maent yn sôn
    A minnau 'n cyson wrando,
Na ŵyr undyn yn y wlad
    Pwy ydyw 'nghariad eto;
Ac ni wn yn dda fy hun
    A oes im un ai peidio.

277

Plannaf esgyll dan fy mron,
    Mi a' i Bumlumon fynydd;
Cadwaf lwyn i'm cadw'r haf,
    Ac yno mi gaf lonydd.
Brysia dithau i gneua ar des
    Dan loches mynwes manwydd.

278

Yn harbwr Cork yr oeddwn
    Ryw fore gyda'r dydd,
'R oedd yno bawb yn llawen,
    'D oedd yno neb yn brudd.

'O Rhisiart,' meddai Morus;
    'O Morus,' meddai Twm,
'Gwell inni riffio 'r hwyliau
    Cyn delo'r tywydd trwm.'

275

Working in the barn with Dad,
    Talking and laughing lightly,
I mentioned marriage — and his eye
    Began to boggle slightly.

276

All around they talk and gossip
    While I just lend an ear;
There's no-one in this country fathoms
    Yet, who is my dear;
In fact, if I have one at all
    Is not now all that clear.

277

I'll plant two wings beneath my breast,
    I'll fly to quest Pumlumon;
I'll seek a grove, when summer's kind,
    And there I'll find oblivion.
Hurry to gather, while the sun's hot,
    Nuts where the low trees beckon.

278

We entered old Cork harbour
    One morning with the tide.
We found the people laughing,
    There no-one moaned or cried.

'O, Richard,' said young Morris,
    'O, Morris, turn about,'
Said Tom, 'we'd better scarper
    Before the storm breaks out'.

279

Pan fyddo'r llan yn llawen
Heb falais na chenfigen,
    Bydd mêl yn tarddu i maes o'r graig,
A ffigys ar y ddraenen.

280

Nid elwyf fyth o'r Rhiwlas,
Ces bendro a phob andras.
    Ni bûm erioed mor ddrwg fy nhrefn.
'Oes baw ar fy nghefn i, Thomas?

281

Mae'r merched yma 'leni
Â'u bwriad ar briodi,
    Heb ddim i'w dodi yn eu tai
Ond hwy ill dau a babi.

282

'N ôl magu hwch 'n y Blaena,
Ac anfon hon i Frysta,
    Er maint a wêl hi yma a thraw;
Yn hwch y daw hi adra.

283

F'anwylyd, f'anwylyd, pa beth yw eich bryd?
Ai dringo pob cangen o'r goeden i gyd?
Y brig sydd yn uchel, a'r codwm sy'n fawr;
Fe geir eich cwmpeini pan ddeloch i lawr.

284

Fy nhaid oedd yn Llanbed' yn berson, ŵr hardd,
Fy hendaid yn Llanfair yn berson a bardd,
A minnau wyf beunydd a chur dan fy mron
Yn glochydd Llanegryn a'm pwys ar fy ffon.

279

With all the parish happy,
No malice here, no envy —
    Honey will gush from every rock,
Figs flock upon the thorn tree.

280

No more will I leave Rhiwlas.
My head spun like a compass.
    Falling, I was badly hurt —
Is my back dirty, Thomas?

281

Girls, mad to get a hubby,
Grab now at any booby;
    Nothing to put inside the house
But wife and spouse and babby.

282

Bring up a sow in Dowlish
And pack her off to Tarshish,
    Whatever she might hear and see —
A sow she'll be and sow-ish.

283

My darling, my darling, what can be your aim?
Is climbing those branches your way to find fame?
The tree-top is high and your fall could mean death.
All your friends will be glad when you climb down
    to earth.

284

My grand-dad was Vicar of Llanbedr once;
My great grand-dad also, priest, bard, and no dunce;
But here am I daily, my heart like a brick,
Llanegryn's old sexton, his weight on his stick.

285

Os wyt yn fy ngweled yn felyn fy lliw
A thithau gyn wynned â'r eira ar y rhiw,
Ystyria di, lencyn, — na fydd yn rhy falch, —
Mai drutach o lawer yw saffrwm na chalch.

286

Cyn i mi yfed nid oeddwn yn gweled
Ffordd yn y byd i dalu fy nyled.
Ond wedi im yfed yr oeddwn yn gweled
Digon i dalu a digon i yfed.

287

Siôn a Gwen sarrug y nos wrth y tân,
Wrth sôn am eu cyfoeth i 'mremian yr a'n';
Siôn fynnai ebol i bori ar y bryn,
A Siân fynnai hwyaid i nofio ar y llyn.

Ond digon synhwyrol y dywedai'r hen wraig
Mai ceirch a gwair lawer i'r ebol sydd raid
I'w gadw yn lysti, a hynny sy'n siŵr, —
Fe helia yr hwyaid eu rhaid 'r hyd y dŵr.

288

Pan euthum i Lundain yn gwisgo hwd du,
'R oedd pawb yn ewyrth neu fodryb i mi;
Ond pan ddeuthum adref yn llawn o ddylêd,
Ewyrth neu fodryb i mi nid oedd neb.

Pan oeddwn gyfoethog cyn myned yn dlawd,
Yr oeddwn yn gâr ac yn gyfaill i bawb;
Pan euthum yn dlawd i fyw mewn dylêd,
Nid oeddwn i'n gâr nac yn gyfaill i neb.

Pan oeddwn gyfoethog mewn llwyddiant a bri,
'Roedd pawb yn y pentref yn plygu i mi;
Ond er pan drodd tynged i'm herbyn yn gas,
I bawb ym mhob twlcyn yr oeddwn yn was.

285

Your skin may be white as the hill snow, fine fellow,
And mine, as you see, is for you far too yellow:
Remember, conceited one, proud as you are
That whitewash is cheaper than saffron by far.

286

Before I got boozed up I just couldn't see
How to pay all the bills they kept sending to me.
But when I got drunk, oh, I knew how to get
More money to booze with *and* pay off my debt.

287

John and Gwen sat, when their kitchen was warm,
Discussing the best stock to buy for their farm.
John fancied a colt, — Gwen didn't respond —
Gwen's choice was just ducklings to swim on the pond!

But yet that old dame, now, was crafty enough;
A colt must have hay, oats, and such dear stuff,
But all that your ducks need to keep them in trim
Is just one small duck-pond on which they can swim.

288

I found up in London, posh in my best gear,
No shortage of uncles and aunties, no fear.
But when I came home full of debts and they heard,
No uncle or auntie would throw me a word.

I was once in the money, before I went broke,
And then all I met were my friends or my folk.
But now I'm in debt, having suffered a fall,
I've got no relations or friends — none at all.

Yes, when I was rich and successful at last,
All in the village bowed down as I passed;
But when cruel fate turned against me once more,
The dwellers in pigstyes would show me the door.

289

Mi euthum â grotan yn druan i'r dre,
Ar feddwl cael llawer o bethau'n ei lle.
Ces halen a hoelion a charrai'n 'y nghlos,
A cheiniogwerth o gannwyll i ganfod y nos.

289

I once took my fourpenny piece to the town,
Thinking to buy many goods there, cash down.
With boot-laces, salt, nails, my money took flight —
And one penny candle to show me the night!

Ffarwel

290

Cariad mab ddaeth ata' i'n greulon
Trwy fy staes ac at fy nghalon;
Minnau glywais chwedl fechan,
F'aeth trwy flaen fy llawes allan.

291

Paid â meddwl, Fenws dirion,
Ar dy ôl y torra' i 'nghalon.
'D wyt ti ond un o ddwy ar bymtheg.
Os pelli di, mi dreiaf chwaneg.

292

Tro dy wyneb ata' i'n union,
Gyda'r wyneb tro dy galon;
Gyda'r galon tro d'ewyllys,
I iacháu carcharor clwyfus.

Moes dy law drwy'r ffenestr unwaith,
Nid oes rhyngom mo'r gelyniaeth.
Y naill ni awn yn ffrins yrŵan
Neu ffarwel byth o heno allan.

293

A thra bo calch ar dalcen plas
Ac ar y g'lomen bluen las,
A thra bo'r ych yn pori'r ddôl,
F'anwylyd fach, ni ddof yn ôl.

Tra byddo dŵr y môr yn hallt,
A bedw gleision yn yr allt,
A thra bo'r frân yn seilio'i nyth,
F'anwylyd fach, ni ddeuaf byth.

Farewell

290

Through my stays, into my heart,
Cruel love once short his dart.
When I heard a certain rumour
Out through my shirt cuff shot that humour.

291

Goodbye — don't think, my former angel,
My heart will break because you're cruel.
You're only one of seventeen lovers —
If you go off I'll try the others!

292

Turn your face, if we must part,
And with your face, Oh, turn your heart;
Turn your heart and turn your will
To heal a captive fallen ill.

Once from your window stretch your hand,
All enmity between us banned.
Let us be for ever friends,
Or let this be how loving ends.

293

While the manor house is white,
While the dove looks blue in flight,
While the grazing cows are black,
My darling, never expect me back.

As long as ocean water's salt,
And birch-trees feel the winds' assault,
And crows build nests at winter's turn,
Darling, I shall never return.

294

Mynnwn gasglu'r niwl a'i hel,
  A'i rwymo mewn sachlenni,
Ar hyd y gweunydd fore a hwyr
  Cyn bario'n llwyr dy gwmni;
Mynnaf hynny, doed a ddêl,
  Cyn cana'i ffarwel iti.

295

Ffarwél i'r merched mwynion,
  Ffarwél i ddrws y plas;
Ffarwél i borth y fynwent,
  Ffarwél i'r garreg las.
Ffarwél i dref Llanddewi,
  Ffawél i'r Eglwys Wen;
Ffawél i'r clochdy uchel
  A'r ceiliog ar ei ben.

294

I would gather morning mists
    That spread across the meadows,
And sew them all up into sacks
    If this would ease my sorrows —
Our parting, so that I must face
    Those single, sad tomorrows.

295

Goodbye, the gentle darlings,
    Goodbye, the manor-house door,
Goodbye, the graveyard lych-gate,
    That rock I'll see no more;
Goodbye to you, Llanddewi,
    Goodbye to Eglwys Wen,
Goodbye, cock and high steeple
    I'll never see again.

Colledion Cariad

296

Nid af ddim i'r gwely heno,
Nid yw'r un 'r wy'n garu ynddo;
Mi orweddaf ar y garreg;
Tor, os torri, 'nghalon fwyndeg.

297

Cleddwch fi, pan fyddwyf farw,
Yn y coed dan ddail y derw;
Chwi gewch weled llanc penfelyn
Ar fy medd yn canu'r delyn.

298

Gwyn fyd y mab a allo weled
Drws ei gariad yn agored;
Fy nghariad i sydd iso'n oeri,
A'r ddaear ddu'n gloëdig arni.

299

Nid oes rhyngof ac ef heno
Onid pridd ac arch ac amdo;
Mi fûm lawer gwaith ymhellach,
Ond nid erioed â chalon drymach.

Haen o bridd a cherrig hefyd
Sydd rhyngof i a chorff f'anwylyd,
A phedair astell wedi eu hoelio, —
Pe bawn i well, mi dorrwn honno.

300

Llawer gwaith y bûm i'n llawen
Yn y fynwent dan yr ywen,
Ac yn fy mreichiau'n dal f'anwylyd
Sy'n awr yn gorwedd yn y gweryd.

Loss in Love

296

Tonight I'll not climb up that stair.
The one I worshipped is not there.
I'll lie instead on her cold stone
And let my heart break there, alone.

297

Beneath the oak-leaves, when I'm dead,
Deep in the forest, be my bed.
On my grave you'll hear the sad
Harp of a yellow-headed lad.

298

Happy the lad who's waited for
And sees his sweetheart's open door.
My love is low and growing cold,
Locked up in the black grave's mould.

299

Earth, coffin and his shroud — these three
Alone are between my love and me;
Further we've often been apart —
Never with so sad a heart.

A layer of earth, pebbled and muddy,
Between me and my darling's body,
And four nailed planks — if you, my heart,
Were sound, all these I'd tear apart.

300

I've been happy with my darling
Often, in the graveyard, lying
With the yew-tree overhead.
That is where she now lies dead.

Yn awr dan frig yr ywen ddulas,
Tra bo'r gwlith yn gwlychu'r gwyrlas,
Gorwedd 'r wyf ar fedd lliw'r lili,
A theimlo 'nghalon drom yn torri.

301

A mi'n rhodio mynwent eglwys,
Lle'r oedd amryw gyrff yn gorffwys,
Trawn fy nhroed wrth fedd f'anwylyd,
Clywn fy nghalon yn dymchwelyd.

Gofyn wnes i'r gynulleidfa,
'Pwy yw'r un a gladdwyd yma?'
Ac atebai rhyw ddyn ynfyd,
'Dyma'r fan lle mae d'anwylyd'.

Trwm yw'r plwm, a thrwm yw'r cerrig,
Trom yw calon pob dyn unig;
Trymaf peth tan haul a lleuad
Canu'n iach lle byddo cariad.

302

Pan oeddwn ar ddydd yn cydrodio
    Â'r bachgen bach glana' 'n y byd,
A welais yn bennaf daplaswr
    Lle byddai'r holl ienctid ynghyd,
Rhyfeddais yn aethus ei weled
    Mor dawel ac isel ei wedd,
Yn curio o gariad merch ieuanc,
    Yn barod i fyned i'r bedd.

There beneath the black-boughed yew,
While the grass is soaked with dew,
I shall feel my sad heart breaking
On the grave of my white darling.

301

I walked the churchyard in my quest
Where countless bodies lay at rest.
My feet led to an open grave.
Up surged my sad heart like a wave.

I approached the mourners, — 'Sir,
Who is she who's buried here?'
To which some heartless man made answer,
'This is the burial of your lover'.

Heavy is lead, boulders are heavy,
Heavy is every heart that's lonely;
Heaviest beneath the sun above
The last 'Goodbye' of those in love.

302

One day, where I found myself walking
    With the handsomest under the sun,
I had thought once the merriest dancer
    Where young ones were gathered for fun.
I marvelled in grief to see him,
    So sad were the glances he gave —
He languished for love of his darling
    Ready to go to his grave.

Hiraeth

303

Tros y môr mae'r adar duon,
Tros y môr mae'r dynion mwynion;
Tros y môr mae pob rhinweddau,
Tros y môr mae 'nghariad innau.

304

Tros y môr y mae fy nghalon,
Tros y môr y mae f'ochneidion;
Tros y môr y mae f'annwylyd,
Sy'n fy meddwl i bob munud.

305

Mae fy nghalon i cyn drymed
A'r maen mwya sy yn y pared,
A chyn llawned o feddyliau
Ag yw gogor mân o dyllau.

306

Ow! fy nghalon, tor os torri.
Pam yr wyt yn dyfal boeni
Ac yn darfod bob yn 'chydig
Fel iâ glas ar lechwedd llithrig?

307

Gwynt ar fôr a haul ar fynydd,
Cerrig llwydion yn lle coedydd,
A gwylanod yn lle dynion;
Och Dduw! pa fodd na thorrai 'nghalon?

Longing

303

Across the sea the black birds fly,
Across the sea the kind lands lie,
Across the sea — all virtues, charms,
Across the sea — my darling's arms.

304

Across the sea my true heart lies;
Across the sea I send my sighs;
Across the sea — there lives my darling,
In my thoughts each night and morning.

305

Heavy as the heaviest stone
In the wall my heart has grown,
And full of thoughts no thought consoles
As a colander of holes.

306

Ow, my heart, break if you must,
Full of sorrow and distrust,
And ending with abandoned hope,
Like blue ice on a sliding slope.

307

Sun on mountain, wind at sea;
Tall grey rocks, but no green tree;
Instead of men the grey gulls crying —
God, what keeps my heart from breaking?

308

Y mae hiraeth wedi 'nghael
Rhwng fy nwyfron a'm dwy ael;
Ar fy mron y mae yn pwyso,
Fel pe bawn yn famaeth iddo.

309

Ni chân cog ddim amser gaea',
Ni chân telyn heb ddim tanna;
Ni chân calon, hawdd iwch wybod,
Pan fo galar ar ei gwaelod.

310

Dwedwch, fawrion o wybodaeth,
O ba beth y gwnaethpwyd hiraeth,
A pha ddeunydd a roed ynddo,
Na ddarfyddai wrth ei wisgo?

Derfydd aur, a derfydd arian,
Derfydd melfed, derfydd sidan,
Derfydd pob dilledyn helaeth,
Ond, er hyn, ni dderfydd hiraeth.

Hiraeth mawr a hiraeth creulon
Sy bob dydd yn torri 'nghalon,
Pan fwyf dryma'r nos yn cysgu
Fe ddaw hiraeth, ac a'm deffry.

Hiraeth, hiraeth, cilia, cilia,
Paid â phwyso mor drwm arna',
Nesa dipyn at yr erchwyn,
Gad i mi gael cysgu gronyn.

311

Y gŵr fo'n glaf, y mae'n ddiamau,
Er cael gwin a'r seigiau gorau,
Y corff ni chlyw un saig yn felys
Os bydd y galon yn hiraethus.

308

Longing possesses me and rests
Between my two brows and two breasts;
Upon my breast I feel its weight
As though to suckle it were my fate.

309

When winter comes, no cuckoo sings;
The harp is dumb without its strings;
The heart can sing no song of gladness
When in its depths lies only sadness.

310

Tell me, you scholars of great learning,
What makes the warp and weft of longing?
What material's woven in it,
That lasts however much one wears it?

Gold and silver will soon wear out,
Silk and velvet need a clout;
All materials have an ending.
This is never true of longing.

Great and cruel is all longing —
Because of it my heart is breaking.
When I lie in bed asleep
Longing wakes me up to weep.

Longing, longing, leave me, leave me,
Do not press so heavy on me.
Move over in the bed, I weep,
Let me have a little sleep.

311

The man who's sick, though given food,
Wine, and fine meals, all for his good —
The body counts sweet feasts as nothing
If the heart is sick with longing.

312

Mae 'nghalon i cyn drymed
    Â'r march sy'n dringo'r rhiw;
Wrth geisio bod yn llawen
    Ni fedraf yn fy myw.
Mae f'esgid fach yn gwasgu
    Mewn man na wyddoch chwi,
A llawer gofid meddwl
    Sy'n torri 'nghalon i.

313

Mi fûm yn gweini tymor
    Yn ymyl Ty'n y Coed,
A dyna'r lle difyrra'
    Y bûm i ynddo erioed:
Yr adar bach yn tiwnio
    A'r coed yn suo 'nghyd, —
Bu bron im dorri 'nghalon,
    Er gwaetha' 'r rhain i gyd.

312

My heart, it feels as heavy
    As the stallion on the hill;
Though wishing to be happy
    I can't, try as I will.
My little shoe, it pinches
    Where you can't guess the pain,
And my mind's many sorrows
    Have rent my heart in twain.

313

I spent one season in service
    Near Ty'n y Coed in Llŷn,
And that's the loveliest landscape
    That I have ever seen;
Trees burgeoned, birds were singing,
    A land without a flaw —
I almost broke my heart there
    In spite of all I saw.

Angau

314

Ar ryw noswaith yn fy ngwely,
Ar hyd y nos yn ffaelu cysgu,
Gan fod fy meddwl yn ddiama'
Yn cydfeddwl am fy siwrna'.

Galw am gawg a dŵr i 'molchi,
Gan ddisgwyl hynny i'm sirioli,
Ond cyn rhoi deigryn ar fy ngruddiau
Ar fin y cawg mi welwn Angau.

Mynd i'r eglwys i weddïo,
Gan dybio'n siŵr na ddeuai yno;
Ond cyn im godi oddi ar fy ngliniau
Ar ben y fainc mi welwn Angau.

Mynd i siambr glòs i ymguddio,
Gan dybio'n siŵr na ddeuai yno,
Ond er cyn glosied oedd y siambar
Angau ddaeth o dan y ddaear.

Mynd i'r môr a dechau rhwyfo,
Gan dybio'n siŵr na fedrai nofio,
Ond cyn im fynd dros lyfnion donnau
Angau oedd y capten llongau.

315

Aderyn bach â'i bluen sidan
A'i big aur a'i dafod arian;
Dacw'r tŷ a dacw'r 'sgubor,
Dacw'r beudy a'r drws yn agor;
Dacw'r dderwen fawr yn tyfu,
A'r man lle mynnaf gael fy nghladdu.

Death

314

Sleepless one night I lay in bed
Thinking about that hour with dread
Because my mind keeps wide awake
Dreading that journey I must take.

I'd wash, and called for basin and water,
Hoping to make that dark night happier;
No drop had touched my cheeks when grim
Death stood at the basin's rim.

I thought I'd go to church to pray —
Surely from there he'd keep away.
Before my knees had left the floor
Death entered though I'd closed the door.

In a safe room I went to hide
Certain he'd never get inside.
That safe room was safe no more —
Death rose up through the solid floor.

I thought I'd row across the sea
Sure he couldn't swim after me.
Before smooth waves and I could meet
Death was the captain of the fleet.

315

Little bird, feathered satin sleek,
With silver tongue and golden beak,
There's the house, the barn beside,
The byre whose door is open wide —
And there the oak whose great boughs wave
On ground I wish to be my grave.

Afterword

Those who require more information about the history of these verses should turn to T.H. Parry-Williams's edition, *Hen Benillion*, which gives full details of manuscript and printed sources. The earliest recorded examples are isolated verses occurring in manuscripts of the late sixteenth century, and it was not until the eighteenth century that any collections were made. It is impossible to date most of the verses themselves with any accuracy. Some clearly are at least as old as the sixteenth century, but the vast majority belong to the seventeenth and eighteenth centuries. It seems that the tradition of composing *penillion* was dying out by the time that their collection had become fashionable, but nevertheless some were certainly still being produced in the nineteenth century, adding to the already vast repertoire which some performers appear to have possessed.

These translations are the fruit of over fifty years' involvement with the *hen benillion*, extending back to the very beginning of Glyn Jones's literary career in the 1930s. This collection first took shape in the 1970s, but Glyn continued to revise and polish his translations until shortly before his death in 1995. Only a handful have previously been published, in two limited edition pamphlets produced by the Gregynog Press, *When the Rose-bush Brings Forth Apples* (1980) and *Honeydew on the Wormwood* (1984), each containing sixteen verses, reprinted together with a few more in *Goodbye, What Were You?* (1994).

Any translator of poetry is constantly faced with the dilemma of choosing between an accurate rendering of the sense of the original verse and a faithful impression of its metrical characteristics. Like many translators who are themselves poets, Glyn Jones has given high priority to the reproduction of metre and rhythm, but not at the cost of accuracy of sense or tone. He has constantly sought to achieve a balance between form and meaning, and I think he does himself an injustice when he states, with characteristic modesty, that some of his renderings are more imitations than translations. Interestingly, most of the revisions which he made to the typescript draft brought his versions closer to the sense of the originals. The reader who has no Welsh can be confident that these translations convey the essential meaning of the Welsh verses, as well as a good deal of their verbal and metrical form.

The relationship between Wales's two literatures was a lifelong concern for Glyn Jones, and although he chose English as the medium of his creative work, he was a fluent speaker of Welsh, and its literature had a pervasive influence on his own writing. The aristocratic art of the medieval strict-metres held a strong aesthetic appeal for him, but more in keeping with his socialist sympathies was the 'people's poetry' of the *hen benillion*, deriving from rural communities like that of his father's family in Carmarthenshire which meant so much to him. The publication of this bilingual collection is therefore a most fitting conclusion to Glyn Jones's splendid literary career. His translations will lead some readers to a better appreciation of the original Welsh, as he hoped, and will be read by others as poetry in their own right.

Dafydd Johnston

About the Translator

Glyn Jones (1905-1995) was a poet, short-story writer and novelist. Born in Merthyr Tydfil into a Welsh-speaking family, his education was entirely in English and he became a teacher in Cardiff and Bridgend. In addition to three novels, three volumes of stories and a posthumous *Collected Poems*, he also published *The Dragon Has Two Tongues* a seminal piece of autobiographical writing which included personal appreciations of writers in both the languages of Wales. This attempt to bridge the two literary cultures is continued in this volume of translations.

About Dafydd Johnston

Dafydd Johnston is Professor of Welsh at the University of Wales, Swansea. He has published extensively on Welsh literature of all periods, including a general introduction, *A Pocket Guide: The Literature of Wales* (University of Wales Press, 1994). His particular interest in translation is seen in three bilingual volumes, *Canu Maswedd yr Oesoedd Canol / Medieval Welsh Erotic Poetry* (Tafol, 1991), *Galar y Beirdd / Poets' Grief* (Tafol, 1993), and *Iolo Goch: Poems* (Gomer, 1993), and in the special number of *Modern Poetry in Translation* (No 7, Spring 1995) which he edited.